Home of the Wildcats

Home of the Wildcats

Perils of an English Teacher

Joan Cutuly

National Council of Teachers of English
1111 W. Kenyon Road, Urbana, Illinois 61801-1096

Grateful acknowledgment is made for permission to reprint Joan Cutuly's previously published poems:

"Wednesday, November 16, 1988, 11:45 A.M.," "The Smokers," and "Brandon" from *Desert Wood: An Anthology of Nevada Poets*, edited by Shaun T. Griffin. Reprinted with permission from the University of Nevada Press. Copyright © 1991 University of Nevada Press.

"The White Piñata," "No Trees Were Destroyed to Create This Poem," "Animal Shelter," and "Teacher in Space" from *California English*, November–December 1990. Used by permission.

"Invisible Paws" and "Rusty" from *Oklahoma English Journal*, Spring 1991. Used by permission.

Project Editor: Michelle Sanden Johlas

Cover Design: Carlton Bruett

Interior Book Design: Doug Burnett

NCTE Stock Number 21306-3050

Library of Congress Cataloging-in-Publication Data

Cutuly, Joan, 1942–
    Home of the wildcats : perils of an English teacher / Joan Cutuly.
        p.   cm.
    ISBN 0-8141-2130-6

    1. English philology—Study and teaching—United States. 2. English teachers—United States—Biography. 3. School prose, American.
    4. School verse, American. 5. Cutuly, Joan, 1942– . I. Title.
PE68.U5C86   1993
428.2'092—dc20
[B]   92-35737
                                                         CIP

428.2092
C991

Tell me how *you are searching, and I will tell you* what *you are searching for.*

Ludwig Wittgenstein

Contents

Preface: The Challenge

On January 28, 1986, I had a dangerously severe case of the flu (the flu—a physical manifestation of spiritual malaise, nature's way of allowing us to drop out for a while). I awoke about the time I ordinarily would have been winding up my second-period English class. Despairing that I had missed the lift-off, I shuffled feverishly into the living room and turned on the TV just in time to see the first replay of that horrifying plume, *Challenger* and its precious crew blown apart into that confused question mark across the sky.

This disaster was a personal tragedy for me. Christa McAuliffe was the only teacher I could name who had ever been given the chance to go beyond the earthly limitations of classroom teaching. Her classroom would be the space that holds the world, and all us earthbound souls would learn without worksheets, scantrons, accountability jargon, cheerleaders, tailbacks, bathroom passes, candy sales, and homecoming queens. Her performance would be a pure blend of science and art, the bonding of form and spirit unfettered by concrete bureaucracies and terra firma burdens of child abuse, teenage suicide, random violence, drug and alcohol abuse, aggressive disrespect, and passive-aggressive apathy. A master teacher would be able to teach masterfully. Christa would achieve what I and so many teachers desire but can never begin to hope for: the chance to be our best.

Maybe that's why every January 28 since then I have asked my students to contemplate the nobility of the challenge Christa and the lost shuttle crew set for themselves, as well as the bureaucratic hubris which took such terrible advantage of them and their ideals. To encourage the positive, I ask each student to write a personal challenge, seal it in a self-addressed stamped envelope, and give it to me for mailing the following January. I also write and mail myself a challenge each year; in 1990, writing *Home of the Wildcats* was it.

For five years, I had been finding it harder and harder to go on. *Home of the Wildcats* was mainly my search for a way to maintain beauty, laughter, intellectual elegance, and personal integrity within a system that not only fosters mediocrity and dishonesty but seems unable even to define its problems. I discovered painfully that, as in the archetypal quest, answers would come only after I had confronted my own weaknesses. Although these confrontations must always be made privately, there was someone to support me before every excruciating mirror. These people, whom I acknowledge here, were my teachers.

I dedicate this book to my mother, Elizabeth Cutuly, who has always challenged me to look beyond myself, and to my father, Dr. Eugene Cutuly, who has always challenged me to look more deeply within.

I also owe an inestimable debt of gratitude to the Editorial Board of the National Council of Teachers of English for accepting the challenge of publishing *Home of the Wildcats,* which may be construed by some as a radical and unwarranted departure from tradition. In fact, I now confess that I sent the brazenly unconventional manuscript as a kind of joke. "Won't this irk The Establishment?" I thought after an exceptionally difficult week. However, if I had been asked to create the ideal champion for my book, it would have been Michael Spooner, NCTE's senior editor. Almost immediately he and his brave Board sent the manuscript to a group of peer reviewers who were at once the most encouraging and most challenging critics I have ever had. These stern folks would not tolerate the slightest whimper of self-pity or the tiniest sliver of arrogance. They were the audience I had always craved; they not only wanted but demanded my best. Like all great teachers, they generated improvement in my work that led not only to artistic insight but to important personal growth. All the while, Michael's empathetic support and suggestions helped me reclaim my badly eroded morale. When it came time for him to turn me over to project editor Michelle Sanden Johlas, I continued to be enthusiastic, but didn't believe anyone could understand the book as well as Michael. Wrong again. If I had been about to die and this book were my child, I would have given it to Michelle without hesitation and with full confidence that it would grow up as well as I could ever have imagined. In short, NCTE's editorial staff renewed my faith that poetic, professional, and personal integrity are still vital forces and are worth fighting for.

But how could I ever have doubted, when over the years so many have remained so encouraging when my faith flickered? I begin by celebrating The Teachers Who Made a Difference:

Rae Chalmers, my grandmother

Mr. George Remetz, Edgewood Elementary School in Edgewood, Maryland

Dr. William French, currently at West Virginia University and previously at the University of Pittsburgh

Mr. Frederick Mayer, University of Pittsburgh

Dr. Thomas Philbrick, University of Pittsburgh

Dr. Joseph L. Grucci, Pennsylvania State University

I also must thank all my students over the years for the constant reminders that the abstract themes of literature grow out of the pain of ordinary people and need to be studied, not for critical exercise, but for their capacity to heal. And special thanks to all those students who granted me permission to use their writing in this book.

Additional thanks to Bill Abrams and Shaun Griffin for their abiding friendship and my "northern exposure"; to Page Benway, Brian Blank, Robert Bonakdar, Helen Lloyd Call, Oscar Fernandez, Patricia Goedicke, Albert Goldsmith, Joe Johnson, X. J. Kennedy, Jenny Kucan, Ken Kucan, Joan Eve Trimble, and Chill Yee for their invaluable contributions to the manuscript; to Patricia Fulwider and Niki Howard for administrative encouragement; to Sally Hellman for her "connections"; to J. E. Morales for my author photo and Frank Brusa for permission to use it.

For the magnificent lessons of brightness in bleak times, my eternal gratitude to Denise Armijo, Rhonda Bauer, Lila Berberet, Carrie Bettles, Candace Bryner, Thomas V. Gaydos, Patricia Goedicke, Karen Haggar, Rosemary Howley, Linda Iafollo, Laura, Harry, Brian, and Ross Ingram, Mary, Tom, and Lydia Karlheim, Jenny Kucan, Bob Luce, Kay McGarvey, Mary Celine Miller, Bev Piggott, Monica Rezaian, Walter Scott, Jean Silvernail, Joan Turner, Tom Whitehead, and Dorothy Wright. Thanks also to The Committee and to Cooch for all the free pencils.

And, of course, thanks beyond words to Dr. Ping for his herbal and verbal tonics and to Dr. A. Wilber Stevens, poet, teacher, editor, critic, and husband who is never without a reason to go on.

The Impertinent Question

. . .?

The president of the United States and other bigwigs should quit worrying about math and science scores in the public schools. They should worry, instead, that students can't read poetry. After all, many great discoveries of our century—from the cellular to the cosmic, from the physiological to the philosophical—were developed and explained through metaphor. For example, Francis Crick and James Watson led us up the spiral staircase of DNA. Albert Einstein took us riding on a beam of light. Less exotically but just as profoundly, psychologist Erich Fromm suggested that our selection of romantic partners may be motivated by the same self-centered drives that dictate selection of a product in the market system.

Poetry is the imagination at work, the transition between the known and the unknown. Poetry, for instance, is the stripping of Darth Vader's mask to reveal the human spirit given over to the machine of state. Poetry is the realization that we are worshiping the ground we walk on to such an extent that we are destroying it. This desecration, as any Native American knows, is unpoetic; this desecration is crazy. Perhaps we all need to learn what Loren Eiseley, paleontologist and poet, realized when he touched a spider's web with his pencil: to the preyless spider for whom pencils have no meaning, he did not exist. That's poetry.

Then there is Carl Jung's revelation of the collective unconscious, the idea that each person's mind is a microcosm of all the universal archetypes. In fact, seeing oneself as a small example of the mythic struggle between Good and Evil may be the supremely important metaphor of our time, the only weapon we have against our social, political, and personal bureaucracies. As Einstein said, "Imagination is more important than knowledge." So, suggests *Home of the Wildcats,* why not push poetry along with science and math?

"It sounds schizophrenic," said the New York literary agent to whom I described this work over the phone. I tried explaining that the schizophrenic and the poet both see unusual relationships, but the poet can order those relationships into metaphor. Unfortunately, her metaphor for money was cold and hard.

I wasn't surprised, of course, for I know that most graduates of the American Public Education System grow up thinking poetry is of the people, by the people, and for the people who want to blow their brains out or perform unspeakable acts of love with a variety of other misfits needing a bath, a haircut, and a good salad.

If only these misinformed graduates knew that they are what drives poets to write, as well as what drives them crazy. You see, I know how both sides feel because I was born a poet to two respectable, friendly, highly educated scientists who enjoy books, plays, classical music, good movies, and educational vacations. However, when I would express my nonconformist poetic nature in any way, there would be one of those family talks. Everyone had an assigned seat: Mom in her chair beneath the print of Renoir's "Girl with a Watering Can"; Dad in his spot on the sofa surrounded by footstool, newspaper, journals, and hot-water bottle; me in the dark corner chair next to the door. "Joan," my father would say, "you are on a collision course." When I went off to college, I would receive with deadly regularity clippings from one periodical or another describing the latest death by oven or alcohol.

Either I was sufficiently warned, cowardly, realistic, not a real poet, or—as I like to remember it—a person of some social and moral conscience. Anyway, I decided to go into teaching. My plan was to save money for a couple of years while experiencing real life, move to the desert, write, and become great. Steps 1, 2, and 3 went off without a hitch. After two years of teaching, I left Clairton High School in Pennsylvania for the place of my poetic heart, Zion Canyon in Utah. I wrote for two-and-a-half months and sold one short story for $5.00. One night a horrendous thunderstorm ripped through the canyon. Across from my room, which smelled like the cheap canned meat I'd had for supper, forked lightning cracked like the hand of God out of the triangular mountain known as The Watchman. I promised that if the storm ever ended I would go back to teaching.

The second time I quit was to get married. One evening I was raking dead grass out of our lawn when Bonnie Barton dropped by. "I can't see you hoeing grass for a living," she said. Bonnie was a tall, tough blonde who wore black leather jumpers with medallions that looked like authentic medieval weapons. One day I had stayed late to grade papers, and Bonnie appeared in my doorway. Her black boots clomped toward my desk. She stood over me. "What's the reason for being good?" she asked in a tone reviving the spirit of the Inquisition. I said what I was supposed to say, and she looked disappointed.

"I guess that sounds like bullshit," I said.

"Yeah," she agreed, pulling up a desk. I don't remember what I said next, but we talked until we became indistinct shadows in the twilight.

Now here Bonnie was to tell me that she had started college and that I shouldn't be raking grass for a living. I began right then to face the truth: my marriage was not right; it was an escape. I lay awake all that night remembering:

"I'll do the play," I had offered with unqualified enthusiasm, the extent of my dramatic flair. It was the late sixties, and the drama coach had just resigned after the black population, about 40 percent of the school, protested *The Barretts of Wimpole Street* as the class play; being butlers wasn't their thing.

The students were talented and devoted, but wild. The play was *Hippiecrites,* my creation based on F. Scott Fitzgerald's "The Diamond as Big as the Ritz." We had music, dancing, gymnastics, exotic lighting, and the potential for a flawless, exuberant performance. We better have; the War-Horses of the faculty were convinced that my warped sense of social justice was going to result in my death and/or dishonor, and they were hoping for the worst.

Ha. I was going to show them, although "I'll do this or die trying" began taking on immediate and profound significance. For one thing, we didn't have much equipment, and we were all learning together. Probably I did most of the learning. I'd say, "Doggone, if only we had some blue filters for those lights." The next day Chauncy and Delmar would walk in with a couple of old shopping bags. "Hey, Miss Cutuly, man, we just happened on some a-them filters." I grew to look upon this method of acquisition as society's contribution to the arts.

Then there were the nightly rehearsals. We had no security in the school, so kids could drop in from the streets. One night I went backstage to chase out the interlopers. I was surrounded in the darkness by hot black bodies, the smell of cheap wine, and the sweetness of burning leaves. The hotness began closing in. Suddenly, Delmar was beside me. He was playing a police officer in our production; having donned his cap, he took my arm and moved me through a path he made in the crowd with his nightstick. "Anyone touches this woman," he said, "deals with me." From that day on, I could walk down the main street of town, day or night, and be greeted, "Hey, Miss Cutuly, man, how you doin', man."

But then came the disaster of dress rehearsal. The rule was that if you skipped practice, you were out. Mitzi, the lead singer, didn't show. She figured she was indispensable. She was. But she was out. I had to do it; they were all waiting to see if I would remain fair under pressure.

Slowly from the wings, Stoney Davenport came to fill in. And nobody could believe it; she was better than Mitzi. She was great!

The next morning, though, as the tardy bell was ringing, Stoney came to say she couldn't go on that night. She was a gospel singer; she only sang for the Lord; she would get a stake through her heart for saving our show. I said I didn't think the Lord would mind this once, that all our hard work would go for nothing without her. I was raving inside with desperation. Delmar and Chauncy had made sure everyone bought a ticket, and my family would be there, front and center, with the administration and faculty. Stoney said she would do it for me.

That night, after the performance, we all stood in the dim corridor between the lockers, applause still pounding through us. All jubilant. Perfect. Except Stoney. And though the production became legendary, I have never been able to atone for my shameful need.

Shortly after came the riots of the sixties. One day I saw boys and girls tearing at each other in the halls and police dogs brought in to get others out of the auditorium. Also that day the principal told my three best students that they should go into the auditorium to reason with their classmates. It was their civic duty, they were told—this from the administrator who tried to pass off a storefront degree.

The three honor students asked me if I really believed what I had said when we read *Hamlet:* that in some ways, Horatio could be thought of as the real hero because he was the only one to preserve his honesty by remaining independent of evil.

I assured them that I really believed it and that they would not be cowards if they tried to maintain order and reason by going to class. I never will forget that moment when Shakespeare was more alive for me than on my trip to Stratford or during Brian Bedford's *Hamlet,* which I loved so much I saw it three nights in a row.

The next year, my little acting company put together a dramatic celebration of black literature and music for Martin Luther King Jr.'s birthday. But at the last moment, the assembly was canceled by the administration for unclear reasons that made both blacks and whites suspect my motives. I could not bear becoming an instrument of disappointment and mistrust. That's when I got married and began writing children's stories.

Bonnie Barton's visit reminded me of my old purpose.

The third time I quit teaching was to work for an insurance company so I would have more time to write. It was also the year I began to attend every available writing workshop. Once John Ciardi slid my life's work back across the table to me. "This is some of the worst poetry I have ever read," he said.

"You mean," I implored, "there's no redeeming quality to it whatsoever?"

Ciardi shook his head; it was odd to see one so direct and vast and fabulous waver. "There is," he said, "real intelligence here. But the poetry . . . it's . . . it's awful."

A few months later, I got lost among trees and stone in Acadia National Park. Not only did I promise to go back to teaching, but to give up drinking and swearing. Back in my cabin, I gasped "Jesus Christ" as I opened a beer. But I did go back to teaching.

This circular commitment to teaching and writing has always puzzled me. Bluntly, I wonder why I have given so much of my life to teaching when I always wanted to be a writer. Well, I agree with Ludwig Wittgenstein: "Tell me *how* you are searching, and I will tell you *what* you are searching for." Therefore, we'll need to go back to the beginning . . . to that moment when "the road less traveled" became "the collision course." The precise moment was a sunny autumn afternoon in 1948. The place was Room 104 of Fifth Street Elementary School in Clairton, Pennsylvania: I said Mother was peeling vegetables.

> I was supposed to say carrots.
> Miss Davidson, fingernails like cold sharp moons
> Touched into her little flat box of gold foil stars
> Stuck one, scissored it, ground one half
> Between her thumb and opaled finger, tongue-tipped the other,
> and pressed it into my forehead . . .

When you're a kid, you don't realize you don't have to accept half stars for what you believe in, so all afternoon I wore that half star as a symbol of my incompleteness. When I got home, the ladies in my mother's garden club said, "Oh, you got a star!"

"No," I confessed, "it's half a star. I said mother was peeling vegetables." The ladies laughed pleasantly and went back to their plants. My mother offered me refreshment, but I chose to go up to my room alone.

I thought of that half star when I first read about Hester Prynne. The lesson had burned its way through my forehead. To get the coveted *A,* I'd have to do it right.

> And round and round and round and round we went
> As Mrs. Cupp's pointer circled above Armand Martin's desk
> His left hand corkscrewed over
> His good white writing paper   WHAP!
> Went the pointer   Armand's ovals
> Took off like planets in a gravity storm
> CRINKLE-PLONK went Armand's paper into the basket.
> "Babies," said Mrs. Cupp, "must go back
> To big wide baby lines."
> And round and round and round we went
> As Armand's big wide baby lines
> Bled in his tears.
> The next day I turned left instead of right and
> Circled back down the hill through the alley
> Behind the church straight onto the weathered bench
> In Skapiks' grape arbor
> Skapiks spoke and cooked in strange fragrances
> Death rocked there in black
> Only my grandmother had them over to her porch
> All morning I sat in the green of patient seclusion
> "You are," my father said, "a blot
> On my character."
> "Why?" asked Mrs. Cupp,
> "Is it because you don't like your teacher?"
> Her face curved like the foot of a bird
> Clinging to its perch.
> "My ovals aren't like the book," I told Mrs. McConnell.
> She was the principal. Her first name was Mazie.
> The bad kids called her Maizin the Raisin.
> "The book," she said, not at all little or dark,
> "The book is by artists and machines."
> My shoes squeaked down the long dim corridor
> Back to Mrs. Cupp's room.

And there you have it: The Day I Became a Blot. My first lesson in metaphor. It might have been easier to be a simile: like a blot. But no, I was a blot. A blot on a collision course.

I've felt fairly depressed about this over the years. In fact, it wasn't until a year or so ago that, while reminiscing about those good old days,

I had a fascinating poetic thought that's cheered me up a bit. I recalled that we used to refer to those little sojourns from our appointed day as "playing hooky." Today it's called "ditching." Now there are a couple of terms whose poetic connotations ought to be examined. Doesn't *hooky* suggest a bit of subtle craft? Actually, the derivation of *hooky* is a Dutch word meaning hide and seek. Kind of a quest theme . . . dodging the dark knight and all. The memory of Skapiks' grape arbor came back, and, feeling downright Waldenesque, I continued my metaphoric meditations.

Ditching, I thought, suggests being fed up, ready to dump it all—out of a feeling of frustration or despair. I don't sense any philosophical motivation to ditching. Dumping is not anywhere close to hiding or seeking.

I wonder if this metaphoric study in contrast is ever the subject of discussion among the governors or education reformers when they get together to chitchat about test scores and the state of things. More to the point, does anybody ever ask the students why—or if—they feel at risk? Nobody ever asked me. How I longed for someone to ask me. Instead, people were always telling me what they thought I needed, even what they thought I was thinking.

In my early years of teaching, I also did that to my students because I was too insecure to admit I didn't know everything, too afraid to show weakness. Then over the years, my study of Lao-tzu and the Chinese mystics made me realize that at night most people look at the stars, never giving any credit to the space that allows the stars to happen. I decided I wanted my classroom to be like Space. But how could I write that as a measurable objective?

> To make my room like Space . . .
> To allow the stars to happen . . .

Talk about a blot on a collision course! So my lesson plan book was always one measurable objective after the other. I even won a couple of awards and was invited to do a number of workshops on teaching writing and literature. But deep inside where I nurtured my secret objectives, I was scared to death of being found out.

Eventually, I quit doing workshops because I felt like a fraud. I mean, to give a successful workshop, you have to say, "My kids love this, and boy, are they ever doing wonderful things." The fact of the matter is that my students never read or write any better than any other students, no matter what methods I use. Furthermore, my students and I argue a lot. There's usually respect, often friendship, occasionally love in the room, but there's a lot of anger, too—the chaos out of which stars are born.

I remember teaching the research paper and insisting on research as opposed to reportage. "You have to get up off your lazy rears and get out there and ask questions," I said at one of the friendlier moments in the discussion.

"*You* wouldn't go ask questions to total strangers," came the challenge.

"Sure I would," I said as I felt another uncertain star beginning to form. And there I was the next morning, pad and pen in hand, crossing the street to the curb where The Smokers always stood, one step beyond the school's right to kick them out for smoking. You know The Smokers—long hair over their sullen faces, faded denim jackets, black concert shirts, and ripped jeans.

"Hi," I said, "I'm Miss Cutuly—from that room right over there on the corner."

They kept on smoking.

"My students are doing a research paper," I went on, chipper as a fool, "and they said I didn't have the nerve to interview people. So anyway, can I interview you?"

"Hey," said one glazed face to the others farther down the line, "some lady's here from Channel 3."

"Hey, no lie, man."

"Hey, lady, interview me."

I was surrounded by hair and denim that wanted to talk. The smoke was killing me.

"Wait," I said, "I'm just Miss Cutuly from the room across . . ."

They started backing off. Then I heard, "Yeah, she's cool."

I was surrounded again.

"So," I began, "I watch all of you guys smoking every morning, and I always wonder why you smoke since we all know it's bad for your health."

"Might as well, man," the glazed one drawled, "we're all going to get blown up anyway."

"Right on, man," they agreed. "Tell her, dude."

"Well," I continued, "what happens on the off chance that we don't get blown up?"

A pause.

Then the same voice, "I guess I'm fucked, man."

Laughter.

I walked down the alley behind the Smokers and saw clusters of students drinking and smoking joints. I didn't report them because I was on assignment, so to speak. Later, I asked why the administration did not recognize the problem, and the answer was that an unspoken agreement existed with the police that the situation be ignored because "time spent filling out the paperwork on the kids wasn't worth it since nothing would be done."

After I described my experience to the honors comp classes, we defined the various problems, analyzed causes and effects, compared and contrasted possible solutions, and applied these research procedures to other projects in the class. The result: Many of the finished papers were still careless, superficial, and disappointing. But when my poem entitled "The Smokers" was published, the class that drove me craziest threw a party to celebrate my accomplishment. Still, I always felt like a failure because what really goes on has nothing to do with measurable objectives.

I always felt like a failure—is that literal or figurative? As a poet, I'm always interested in when and how a group of words becomes a poem. When and how did I come to write this book? There are those moments when a string of literal words or events turn to poetry. As for this book, its genesis was on a bright May day, about four in the afternoon. I had just gotten home from school. I was exhausted—no, make that demolished. The place was the top step in my house, the point at which the downstairs living area becomes the loft where my study is. I sat there with my cat, cd for Civil Disobedience, purring like mad beside me. Space had never been so dark. Here's what had happened:

About a month before, one of my eleventh-grade English assignments was to improve things in the community by using problem-solving methods we had discussed. One group decided to start an organization called S.A.V.E., Students Against Vandalizing Education. The plan was to clean up the campus, then eventually to fix it up with murals and cool stuff. Two major complaints had always been that the bathroom stalls had neither doors nor toilet paper. The doors had been removed because they were always being torn off. Students thought that if there were pride in the school, vandalism would cease. Human dignity could be restored, and possibly even some toilet paper along with it.

The initial plan was to meet with all the gang leaders and ask that the campus become a neutral and respected turf. First, the class elected Jim Bigelow president. Then it decided that the handwriting on the wall suggested the need for a little newspaper which would give the unheard and unsung a voice. I even found a connection in a local placement agency so we could offer worthwhile jobs to S.A.V.E. members.

The meeting with the gang leaders was set. I had informed the dean but asked that he not attend. That morning, Jim arrived. He looked as if he had been drinking the night before; could I talk to the guests? I'm in this too deeply to quit, I said to myself, and I'm going to get stuck. Anyway, I talked to the leaders—Bloods, Crips, 28th Street, Little Locos, KBs, Stoners; Black, Asian, Hispanic, White—all staring at me and each other with complete bemusement. The idea of the newspaper, however, caught their attention—a voice for their people. In twenty-four hours *all* vandalism on campus stopped. The head custodian and his staff were awed and relieved. They no longer spent their mornings painting over the graffiti scrawled across the campus. In the next three weeks, we put out two newspapers with articles by the "gangsters" explaining why S.A.V.E. was a great organization. The head custodian even wrote an article outlining what he would do with the money he saved on paint: lavatory doors along with such things as new planters in the quad. And Jim Bigelow? Jim never failed me. He didn't have a hangover that morning. He came to school because he didn't want to let S.A.V.E. down. He had promised. It was several hours after our meeting that I found out his father had died the night before.

Our organization grew, and we had big plans for the following year. I asked for an English class of about thirty-five "at-risk" (the operative word for Administration) students so we could put out the paper and develop the concept of S.A.V.E. on a regular basis. I also requested the privilege of my own room all day, even though other teachers had to share. I thought this fair because of the enormous energy required by the project. First, I was told that every student needed the traditional credit in English 1, 2, and 3. Then I was also told I was no better than anybody else. Actually, I felt worse than anybody else because I had failed. I knew I couldn't keep up the rigorous responsibility of S.A.V.E. along with five other classes (three different subjects) a day. When I explained this to the students, they understood and decided, during summer vacation, to plead their case before The Administration. In fact, a few of their parents went along. The Administration had always stressed the importance of parental involvement, but I guess this involvement was not the right kind. I wasn't there because I had already been given my answer, but I was told one parent got kind of rough around the edges. Anyway, the project was again rejected. Several years later when the bitterness of denial finally abated, I asked one administrator why my requests had been denied. He looked at me with eyes like hot bullets. "You set me up," he said. Meanwhile, I had watched as one by one the S.A.V.E. gang dropped out of school, and vandalism by the voiceless resumed.

I wrote these thoughts in a long letter to President George Bush after he outlined his education goals in his 1990 State of the Union Address. These goals seemed to me to reflect a disastrous lack of understanding of the state of American public education. Not even a hint of poetry. The response from the Department of Education thanked me for my interest: "It is concerned citizens such as you who will help bring about the restructuring of education so vital to the future of this great nation." Enclosed from the U.S. Secretary of Education were "Remarks Prepared for Delivery Before the U.S. Department of Education Forum," remarks "EMBARGOED FOR RELEASE: 11:15 A.M. (EST)/ Wednesday, January 18, 1989." I studied the metaphors in these prepared remarks. And not surprisingly, the plan was to do more for "the young people who most need help in reaching the first rung of the ladder of success." There was also, from the White House Press Secretary, "For Immediate Release, February 26, 1990," our "NATIONAL GOALS FOR EDUCATION" in which

> The Governors urge the National Assessment Governing Board to begin work to set national performance goals in the subject areas in which NAEP (National Assessment for Education Progress) will be administered. This does not mean establishing standards for individual competence; rather, it requires determining how to set targets for increases in the percentage of students performing at the higher levels of the NAEP scales.

Ladders and targets! Gasp!

> And of our dreams might we say
> Once we came from a small place
> Robed in the textures of tough flowers
> And morning and evening were as two hands

> And of our efforts might we say
> The world turns on weak ankles
> And morning and evening are as possessions
> Possessed by their own dispossession.

Uh oh, am I whining? Being a martyr? Becoming the clichéd little person against The Bureaucracy? These interpretations amuse me, especially when I am also called arrogant, elitist, or a snob who thinks she has all the answers. These terribly literal accusations are not even remotely related to a blot on a collision course. But maybe I better get literal here before my identity becomes even more hazardous to my health.

As I said, the moment on that step between my living room and my writing room was the day this book was conceived. I had failed to become a strong enough voice for the voiceless who were, in many ways, myself as a child. On that step, I remembered seeing my first bluebird. I was home for lunch in first grade, a gray day, when my mother gently pointed out this small bluebird in the backyard, not a jay but a real bluebird, bluer still as it flew against the gray. Back in school, I crayoned my dittoed cardinal blue. "Oh, my, class," Miss Davidson said as she held up my paper, "someone doesn't know red from blue."

Then I thought of Avanalist Jackson, a tall, reedy, black boy in fourth grade. Avanalist Jackson wore thick, black-rimmed glasses, tiny striped jerseys, and huge dungarees suspended over his shoulders with black mill hunk suspenders. Avanalist Jackson was always lost in *More Streets and Roads* and always the last to get picked for kick ball. He never had a partner in dance class because there weren't enough black girls. On my step, I remembered the day Avanalist Jackson got picked to demonstrate the buzz step we were being taught for square dancing. All alone in the center of the playroom, music blaring, sun streaming through the high windows, Avanalist Jackson spun magically beyond dance, face turned up to the high windows, bottle-bottomed glasses glowing rose gold. That is the only beautiful memory I have of my first five years of school, and it is what I clung to, alone there on the step with cd. At that moment, my heart broke with The System forever.

The System. How do I talk about The System without sounding like a middle-aged hippie staring into the sun? Not long ago I was observed by a principal as my creative writing students read a group poem which was trying to define the chaos known as changing classes. We were attempting to decide which was real: the minutes of chaos or the periods of order, and how the two relate to each other. The poem contained some of THOSE words, the four-letter ones that pepper the language of contemporary America. I was told the next day that this had to stop. "No problem," I said, although I suggested that by eliminating street language from the classroom, we are not confronting the problems of the street. After all, language is thought; you are what you think.

"The fact remains," came the reply, "that if a parent calls to complain, I can't protect you." The truth is, this principal did want to protect me, as well as himself. We understood each other's points, yet The System prevailed. Trembling inside with rage, I went home and wrote.

The Word
for my Creative Writing students

I got the word today.
There are to be no more
Of *those* words spoken in my classroom.
We must write creatively without them.
When the street runs you down and calls you dirt,
I must say brush it off,
I'm clean, I don't live there anymore.
I must say what your father calls you
Is not fit for my classroom,
What your mother says to you can get me
Fired should I allow you to tell your pain here
Though this may be the only place you have to tell it.
So snap your anger back into your pencil box.
Retract your inky courage
And your insights.
I got the word.
My job is on the line
The line we'll all toe
The line we've all learned to speak
That straight and narrow line
The starting line leading right to the finish line
We're off at the sound of the gun
Never mind that someone is killed
In the parking lot during the game—
A few hours later, team and band are lining up at Disneyland.
The bottom line is I got the word.
But how, I wonder, will I reach you now,
Throw you the line that lets you know I know
The Freitag Pyramid is higher and colder than Everest?
Tonight I watched the story of Mother Teresa again.
She walks without fear among the eyes
Staring out of time before The Word.
I know Mother Teresa never takes God's name in vain,
And that she doesn't know where her next dollar is.
I swear I'm soft and that my house is big and warm,
That I fight becoming overweight,
That I'm no saint
Having already been to the other place
Where the only words are empty bottles
And thin papers of weed,
Hieroglyphics of hypocrisy

Cool, tough, rebellious:
They'd never get me . . . they . . .
But there were more antecedents than I imagined,
And I kept walking through a night that lasted years
So I wouldn't go to sleep
Until in a sober moment I heard
The cries of children that were me.
I cast my line across the night.
The line became a bridge.
I crossed out of the hands of fathers,
Out of the weaknesses of mothers
Into the courage of children.
But this morning I got the word.
The bridge is gone. I am grown up.
Alone
In this four-letter place
Where anger is tidy
Fists are tears
Fire is wrong
And I dream of traveling to the bottom of the world
In a very small and desperately open boat.

I have always read and written, believing that through those acts it will be possible for me to retain my soul. I first learned this from Mr. George Remetz, my sixth-grade teacher. I hated school—except for sixth grade and Mr. George Remetz. He read us *Count Luckner, The Sea Devil* by Lowell Thomas. During World War I, the count outfitted a Norwegian fishing vessel with guns, then lured American and British naval ships into range. But even though he did substantial damage to our side, the count did not believe in killing. He took his victims on board, treated them with generosity and respect, and ultimately left them where they could be rescued.

Sometimes Mr. Remetz would read away the afternoon. And at the same time we savored one book, we couldn't wait for the next. After the count, however, we voted, and by unanimous decision, heard it all again.

The count had been our enemy, but we loved him.

It was the beginning of imagination.

Then there was *Victory* by Joseph Conrad. Another book report due for Miss Wilson. The traditional Wilson Book Report: twenty-five to thirty pages of retelling the story. Miss Wilson taught senior English, and students dreaded her book reports from the moment they set foot in high school—earlier if the epic terror filtered down further. Six a year, and I had made it through five. I'd gotten 95 percent on all of them, although I had no idea what I'd done 95 percent of. Rarely did anyone get higher than 95 or 96 percent, and competition to break the grade barrier was keen.

Then came *Victory.* It would be the last Wilson Book Report. Kids were talking forty, maybe forty-five pages. Everyone but me. Forty-five pages on *Victory.* No. I wasn't going to do it—this commitment based on the tenderest of compassion for Axel Heyst looking out on the charred ruins of his skepticism: "Ah, Davidson, woe to the man whose heart has not learned while young to hope, to love—and to put its trust in life!" So simple. So elegant. So gravely beautiful. One-and-a-half pages. And they were my thoughts, not a retelling.

The next day as Wilson read out our grades, the class waited. "Cutuly . . ." She paused, pulled at her three wool cardigans, and surveyed the class as if she were looking for a new student. "Cutuly, 99."

It was the dawn of character.

Increasingly, however, the question for me is not how can I retain my character within The System, but is it possible to do so? Several years ago, my father wrote me a note that helped.

> Dear Joan:
> Many years ago I dabbled in endocrine research. From this I learned a lesson. On the basis of certain known data, I would set up experiments to prove that, logically, only *one* result could be expected. More often than not, I was amazed to discover that the result was shockingly unexpected.
> At first, I would be upset, frustrated, and even angry. I would question the tests, look for errors, try other methods to prove what I had wanted to prove. To no avail!
> When, finally, I accepted the truth, I found that actual facts were more exciting, enlightening, and productive than anything I could have arranged to happen.
> Such acceptance brought contentment, joy, and new and refreshing outlooks. The rewards far exceeded anything I could have realized from the narrow, restrictive, and unimaginative concepts I had set out to obtain.
> How well *you* have proved my point.
>
> > Dad

My mother also sends me notes, praising my perseverance and regretting that with 2,300 miles between us we can't have as many of our long talks during which we always "solve the world's problems." I have learned much from this remarkable and intelligent woman who gave up her zoology career to make a home for our family. What patience it took! I remember a conversation we had more than thirty years ago. I was lounging as only a teenager can while Mom was getting dinner. I mentioned a vague idea I had heard in biology class: Ontogeny recapitulates phylogeny. Mom had lots of thoughts that were clearly and excitingly beyond the uninspired instruction of the coach who ran us through the biology book. Suddenly, my role in the entire evolutionary process as a person, as a link, as a small world, occurred to me—and my poetic soul was born. Those weighty, pregnant years of adolescence ended, and I slid into the brightness of the world.

Still, I was never able to make my folks sure about all this poetry business until I sent them what has since become the second part of this book, a poetic narrative of one day in my life as a teacher.

"We never really realized what you go through," my mother said.

Then several months later, the phone rang. "Your mother and I have been talking," my father said. It was 7:10 Sunday morning. I was still asleep. Phantoms crept up on me. They had been talking. What collision course was I on now?

"We think," he continued, "your book should have an introduction for people like us. You need to tell people this is not an easy book to read. There's not the kind of sex or violence people see on TV and in the movies. It's real. But this is a book that should be read. People need to know they must take the time to understand what is going on."

I was feeling real good. But then my father went on. "There's not enough hope in your book," he said. "People don't want doom and gloom." And he told me the story of Dr. Osler, the great physician who told a woman that all was not hopeless despite the fact that all other doctors said her husband was going to die. The man died, and when Osler saw the woman one day, he hid in a doorway—but the woman had spotted him. She ran up and thanked him for what he had done. Osler was dumbfounded. But the woman said that in her gravest hour, he had given her the hope which got her through. Well, it's a fabulous story. And I get the point. Still, I find it hard day after day to face not death but the lives of children who are ridiculed, beaten, molested, seduced by drugs or materialism, and generally disregarded by a system that exists for the sake of its own order while proclaiming to live for their creative development; children who are treated with so little respect that they are graduated for filling in blanks and selecting from other people's multiple choices.

"If only you can help just one," my mother always reminds me, "it will be worth it."

I know I have helped one, no doubt many—just as all you other teachers out there have. And our generous and blessed reward is that we are often inspired and nurtured forever by the bravery and resilience of these children passing so briefly through our lives. I'll never forget going to a home to pick up a drum set for a play rehearsal. There was nothing in the living room but the set of sparkling red drums, a big TV, and a three-legged chair. Nor will I forget the day Stoney Davenport burst into tears for no apparent reason. It was her birthday, and her mother hadn't even remembered to wish her "happy birthday." Yet out of these children came the miraculous hope of commitment to art and to one another. But after the show, what?

And what did I save with S.A.V.E.? Didn't I just confirm that all the problem-solving techniques in the world don't really work? How and why did I fail to communicate the need for special help in dealing with the "at risk"?

I hesitate . . . would the reader be willing to engage in a daring experiment with metaphor . . . a thought from a blot . . . an unconventional analysis of our nation at risk . . . ? I fear my spiritual wildcatting may alienate, but what have I got to lose; nothing else is really working. Besides, as Jacob Bronowski suggested in *The Ascent of Man*, "That is the essence of science: ask an impertinent question, and you are on the way to the pertinent answer." Well, here goes. Hold on to your tolerance . . .

Could it be that current attempts to reform education are ineffective because The Reformers don't understand the state of being "at risk"—or even that "at risk" is not really an accurate description of the students in question? The correct term, as used by the students themselves, is "fucked." Perhaps contrasting the literal *at risk* with the metaphoric *fucked* may yield a pertinent answer. Let's begin by taking a close look at the language. Like most literal terminology, *at risk* is an intellectual concept incapable of encompassing the emotional world of its metaphoric synonym, *fucked*. Because language reflects one's state of mind, we might conclude that The Reformers are not conscious of the feeling of intimate violation experienced by those who drop out of, or don't believe in, The System. And what is this feeling of intimate violation? It is the feeling of alienation experienced by anyone who feels helplessly exploited by another human being—fucked. Now why do people exploit each other? A desire for power because they feel threatened? Ignorance of the other person's feelings? Repetition of the pattern of abuse? Any one of these amounts to having been fucked and then perpetuating the behavior. This is a terrible cycle we're just beginning to confront as a nation, a cycle that defines in large part the problems in our schools.

But, The Reformers insist, this is the cycle they are attempting to break. They want to rescue the "at risk." Read, they claim, any of their

Mission Statements and School Objectives anywhere in the country, and you will see that they want to save the Lost Sheep. But, I point out, to rescue any lost sheep, the shepherd has to go to where that sheep is. How many Reformers ever leave the State House or Ed Central and enter the Land of the Lost?

Among my first-period junior English themes last year, I received a paper from a student who said he felt like "Jeff Daumer just before the man would slauter one of his victims. In my case my first victim would be my first period teacher." Over the years, I've chosen to handle many bizarre papers alone. But the student who wrote this one had been a chronic and insidious instigator of unrest all year. Every teacher knows the type. The Player of the System, the Con Artist, the kid who communicates that complex mixture of hostility, feelings of unworthiness, and a desperate need for attention in a passively defiant refusal to pass the class.

When this student was questioned, the dean and campus police found a picture of Jeffrey Dahmer in his notebook. He was suspended for three days, then for ten more days pending admittance to the school for special discipline problems, which had been closed due to overcrowding. The police were not permitted by law to investigate, because the student said he wanted to kill me instead of saying he was going to kill me. I, however, was required by law to fill out a paper describing all the assignments the student would be missing in my class, even though I had been told he would be removed from my class "at the very least."

I was also told that in a conference with the dean, the boy's grandmother said that the neighbors love her grandson and that all his problems in school are "because of the niggers."

When I was given to understand that returning the young man to our school had not been completely ruled out, I went to the superintendent. He said that the boy was "entitled to due process" but promised to resolve the matter as soon as possible, and that I should feel free to call him in a couple days. I phoned his office three times, but he never returned my calls. After several months of watching the bushes and shadows, I learned by chance that the student, who was eighteen, had opted right away for adult education and that I had probably agonized for nothing. I could never understand why the Administration in my school was not aware of the facts.

This case is a prime example of The Reformers at work. How much effort—administrative, instructional, secretarial—must have been expended on this student over the years. Yet along the way, no direct effort was made to get at the root of the problem. He, like so many other disturbed young people, was simply kept in school so he could graduate. Still, at eighteen, he was so credit-deficient that he had very little, if anything, to gain by following school or classroom procedures. In fact, he entertained himself by intimidating and undermining. And attitudes like his are an increasingly frightening factor in many public schools.

Teachers who are motivated by the likes of William Faulkner's Sam Fathers remember that we must be "scared" but not "afraid." Yet it's difficult to enjoy the challenge of making "The Bear" rise up with drama and meaning before your students when the shock of recognition has become a live wire. More and more the emotional energy of teachers is spent enduring rather than prevailing along the paper trail leading to a 90 percent graduation rate, that schizophrenic trail on which our goals are to "make learning fun" for the disturbed and apathetic while trying to make learning meaningful for the gentle and aspiring.

We who want to prevail go on in spite of the price too often paid for excellence. Christa McAuliffe, of course, is the universal symbol of death by The System. And for me there is also my friend of twenty-two years who recently got kicked in the mouth while trying to break up a fight in her art room. Back in the sixties, we used to joke about the fact that I'd once overheard one counselor say to another, "This kid's a loser. What can we do with him?"

"Ah," said the other, "just stick him in art."

In another art room just several years ago, when a student stood up to pledge allegiance to the flag, a gun fell out of his pocket and went off . . . "with liberty and justice for all" . . . wounding only a wall. The next year, we were required to post in each classroom signs warning that "arson, battery, selling of controlled substances, robbery, extortion, and carrying weapons will be subject to PERMANENT EXPULSION!" Some video cameras have been installed to watch parking lots and halls; metal detectors are in place at the entrance to sporting events.

Why do so many administrators remain oblivious to the fact that so many classes are chronically disturbed by the same children all teachers *and* all students have identified as problems since elementary school? Why are these students merely pushed through The System? Consider the case of my colleague who confiscated a cellophane bag of candy which a student persisted in rattling. The teacher said the girl could pick up the candy after school. After class, the dean came by with the student to retrieve the candy. This is a slap in that teacher's face, but to have to take issue with the dean over a cellophane bag is absurd and demeaning. Do we say that the winner here is the student, the loser is the teacher, and the dean just goes back to his office? Or do we ask who is "fucked"?

Nor does the ridiculous find balance with the sublime. For on the other side is the tragic. Take the story of Mr. Clarence Piggott, renowned in my district for his devotion to his students and his genius for teaching through inspiration, reassurance, and expectation. One morning in 1982 just before school, Mr. Piggott was shot dead in his classroom by one of those students who had come to feel so fucked that he couldn't bear anyone's faith or help. While doing a poetry workshop at the prison nearly nine years later, I suddenly realized I had come face to face with this great teacher's killer.

Invisible Paws

Night moves among vowels locked tight
In the unmanicured yard, the unretractable
Claws of all the cats who ever lived
Wired round the top of the Cyclone fence,
Eye of the forest of yucca and Spanish bayonet.
Straight up an early half moon
Like the lost navel of the woman inside every man
Where remorse goes constantly in and out of
That one-way door securing the boy
Who emptied himself from the drawer of his father's guns
Into the astounded heart
Of his psychology teacher's unremitting kindness.
Now poems spread like cracks
Through the young man's shatterproof eyes,
And the teacher's widow moves across town to a new home
She will keep gentle with grandchildren

Oh someone has stolen all the cats from their claws
Invisible paws prowl the still desert air.

So just who is "at risk"? And in this culture that adores winners, just who is winning? I don't think for one moment that the student who took Jeffrey Dahmer as his hero is the winner. Nor would I confer winner status on my union representative who said of The Process, "Well, it's not the best way to handle things, but at least he's out of your class. And that's the first step. Of course, if the kid really is crazy, he walks into your room, he shoots you, you're dead—and then what?"

What is going on here? Isn't The System, after all, just a web of protection for those who are afraid of getting fucked? Cover your ass, right?

In my most cynical moments, I can't help wondering if The Reformers really want to solve the problem. As people, they deplore the absurdity of The System. As Reformers, however, they simply observe or administer The Process. They play the Graduation Game the same way the "at risk" play it. Just keep it all moving toward Graduation. And they both play the game because they feel threatened by each other, as well as by the laws that constrain them. The Reformers want to protect themselves and their jobs from the threats posed by the "at risk"; the "at risk" reduce The System to a joke the same way The System has reduced them to scores and measurable objectives. Wouldn't we be correct in saying, then, that The Reformers and The Players are equally at risk . . . lost within The System . . . alienated by that which they don't understand and those who don't really care about them . . . fucked.

Maybe what appears to be stark contrast could be more accurately understood through comparison.

"To be, or not to be, that is the question." Hamlet can fight for right and die, or sell out and live. This, like the ironic relationships of The Reformers and those they would reform, is the tension of poetry, the fabric of tragedy. All poets are Hamlet: the voice of the voiceless, the soul of the alienated, the savior of the "at risk," the weapon of the "fucked."

I have often thought, too, that the scholars who discourse at length about the ribald, rude, and bizarre characters in *The Canterbury Tales* would feel so alienated by those types up close and personal that they would not last the week in many contemporary public school class-rooms. There is an alarming gap between what many people think and what they are willing to feel.

Could it be that if we were all less afraid of revealing our at-risk feelings, we could have more productive communication? By this I mean we should not be afraid of, or put off by, our own personal metaphors or the personal metaphors of others. We should drop the jargon of The System and reach out from our poetic natures. If this seems a simplistic answer, remember that the meaning of any metaphor is in the ever-widening circles of suggestion that ripple from its central image.

And I suppose that as long as I'm in the impertinent mode, I might as well offer a plan to those devoted to effecting reform in our schools. I call my plan The Poetics of Educational Reform. This plan came to me as I was administering one of The Tests—you know, The Tests that give us The Scores. I was reading an extra copy of the test and looking at the "at-risk" children before me. "Stop," I'd say when the monitoring instruc-tions told me to do so. Then, "You may begin," and they'd all set themselves to bubbling in the choices that would tell us all where we stood. After two-and-a-half hours, I wanted to scream, "Stop! No, I really mean *Stop . . . Quit . . . Leave.* Get out of here while you can. This is crazy." Of course, I didn't, but the "at-risk" child within shrieked, "Gave up on me, didn't you? Liar! Coward! Same as all the rest!" And I thought of the previous year's state competency exam which asked the deaf students across the hall to "Discuss your favorite music." I also recalled the administrator who confided, not entirely in jest, "If I ever really thought about all this, I'd probably go home and shoot myself." This was the administrator who gave us teachers copies of The Test ahead of time so "we would know the areas of emphasis."

As I collected the #2 pencils, a small, pink girl remarked, "These tests are, like, so totally dumb."

"An inspired simile," I replied.

"Huh?" she asked absently, digging out an eyelash curler from her purse.

Now, don't get me wrong. I believe in the Classics, the Basics, Universal Values, and Discipline. After all, show me a poem that doesn't rise out of that ground, and I'll show you a greeting card verse. No, my point is that The System is not a space that allows stars to happen. There's no way you can equate stars and scores. Scores are too literal; scores do not represent the union of the intellectual and emotional; scores have nothing to do with poetry. Scores have no soul.

If you're alienated or annoyed by all of this, at least understand that the anger you are feeling is what a blot feels all of its life, a lifetime of anger and alienation that leads to ditching, to being "at risk" . . . to cutting down a sixty-year-old palm tree and not knowing why it was wrong.

Palm

If the tree had been a person
It would have been ready to retire
But the old palm seemed destined to weather anything
Having already survived
The Big Depression
Three wars going on four
The Sexual Revolution, Civil Rights Movement
Splitting of the atom
Bobby Soxers, Flower Children, Preppies, Yuppies
Alcohol, Weed, Speed, Ludes, and Crack
Yes, the old tree, its bark like a tough hide,
Stood forever, as we knew it,
Out back of Main at the edge of the quad.
Oh, the winning seasons and the losing
All our living and our dying were one
To the high old tree
Whose leaves like great gentle hands

Grasped the mysteries of wind,
Secrets which we, creatures of the concrete,
Never quite saw.
Only yesterday teachers taught around it
Facts of a bold blue world
Recorded on the bleached and matted spirits of trees.
True, the old palm did cast only the slenderest of shade
And who among us does not wish to abide in his own brilliance?
Yet who today is so sure, the old palm found down in the breaking
    light
Great gentle hands windless for eternity
Chest-high stump torn ragged—a blunt, unschooled cut—
"Seniors Rule," it says in white paint
On the windows above the bike racks
Two district trucks here to slice up the remains for hauling.
The perpetrators must have planned the stunt yesterday
A dare? A prank? Thoughtless bravado? Just another class crime?
They hung around, treacherous hands on the old trunk
Small conspiratorial breaths
Mingling skyward with the lunch laughter
The ignition of a Spree
A first kiss of a first love
Trusty leaves calling for us like a rusty ocean
Across our private deserts
But our hands were filled with Holy Hosannas
The sun was in our faces
And our fast feet dared not feel
The trembling of aged roots beneath the pavement
Of our ways.

Should we expect otherwise? Remember when the fabulous physicist Richard Feynman dropped the O-ring material from *Challenger* into his glass of ice water? We all learned the hard way that facts are simple and clear, but we simply don't want to look at them. The maddening frustration is that Christa McAuliffe is gone, and the voiceless remain "at risk."

But back to The Poetics of Educational Reform. Instead of excluding the "at risk" from the reform process, why not include their points of view? To this end, I offer Part 3 of this book, the ReACT Practice Test. I think all legislators and education reformers should have to pass both the ACT and ReACT tests before they are eligible to reform. I was going to include the answers to the ReACT, but the answers aren't in the back of the ACT, are they?

So how should you prepare for the ReACT Test? Reading a variety of classic and contemporary poetry is most important. Get the feel of the language. Have fun. Don't worry if you don't "get it" entirely. Above all, don't put any scansion marks above the lines. Read the poems as if you were listening to music, and read each one slowly five or six times. Let the poems wash over you like light. The ideas will come. In between reading sessions, pay attention to all jargon and slang; separate the literal from the figurative, and meditate upon the metaphors. If you have a sign on your wall that says, "Stop and smell the roses," take it down. Replace it with cubist or surreal art. See and think in new ways.

Then pretend it's the first day of school. The teacher says, "For tomorrow, look at the space around a stone and write about the experience."

Mutter under your breath, "This lady is crazy." Ask, "How long does this have to be?" When the lunatic woman says length doesn't matter, become annoyed, then bored. Roll your eyes in disgust. Wait a minute and ask, "What do you really want on this?"

She will give you the "Introduction" to *Desert Notes: Reflections in the Eye of a Raven* in which Barry Lopez describes driving his van across the desert, getting out of the driver's seat, and letting the van go on alone as he sits in the passenger seat wondering who that guy was who used to drive the van.

Become totally ticked off by this ridiculous assignment. Say to the teacher, "This assignment is really stupid. I'm going into Education Reform. I can't be messing around with this stuff." When the teacher smiles without responding, ask, "Can I have a pass to my counselor? I want to get out of here."

Tremble inside and hate that teacher as she pulls from beneath her lesson plan book a copy of the Zen koan about the professor who goes to learn about Zen from the great master Nan-in. As Nan-in serves the professor tea, he keeps pouring as the cup overflows. Finally, the professor points out that the cup is indeed "overfull." Nan-in tells the professor he is like the cup: "You are full of your own opinions and speculations. How can I show you Zen unless you first empty your cup?"

Think that this teacher might not be as dumb as she looks.

But before you get overconfident again, read on . . .

The Day

Somewhere

between the tenth and twentieth billion year of existence a hand from the forty-seventh year of its knowledge lifts the light switch in an English Department workroom

and morning begi . . .

Oh no

Someone has taken the clock—
the rebel Accutrex—
that suddenly began running in reverse last week
to the bell order of students who never get any older
or wiser.

"Look," people had exclaimed,
"The clock is running backwards."
"How do we know we exist?"
"At the moment real time and clock time meet
we will all be drawn past the event horizon
of this place into an even blacker hole."
As bells rang the clock quips lapsed into routine,
but she had already fallen in secret, passionate kinship
with the big round white-faced Accutrex,
its black appointments
and chipper little red hand
running back forty-two seconds to the institutional minute,
never quite getting there,
time beating her heart into minds
run by clocks of their own . . .

Three years ago she had requested a lectern
which was ordered
put on back order
arrived
got lost in The Warehouse
had a tracer put on it
actually wasn't ordered
no, was in fact ordered but
delivered to the wrong school
"Not a good teaching tool anyway,
you'll get behind it
and lose touch with your students"
was however reordered
though not in this year's budget so
will really be ordered

next year
which was last year

But within days, the clock . . .
it had hurt no one
they all have watches
she could have taken it home
let it run,
delighted in its foolish inconsistencies—
"Oh, my brave clock," she mourned, "I should have known . . ."

suddenly curving like the mind of myth

                                                      the hand
     dislodges and chucks the big blue painted-over screw

                                             then moves on

     to the Canon copier . . .

under the flap—

MRS. CROCKER'S POETRY UNIT REQUIREMENTS

During this unit, you will be given "recipes" for writing poems. These will be graded then placed in a notebook. In the upper left corner of each paper, identify the assignment by its name and number. If it is patterned poem #5, then write PP#5. I will **not** grade anything that comes in without **all** of the necessary information.

curving like the mind of space

                                             the hand
          pops Mrs. Crocker's Recipes
into the microwave

                         The copier is jammed—
                         From chalk dust she was born
                         To chalk dust she returns . . .

BOYS   lockered hall   GIRLS
                              keys/door
          desks in rows like minds of metal
          old summers tacked onto bulletin boards
          shadows of new leaves kaleidoscoped across the clean green boards

in the silver trough, all her unwritten poems—dust
of a presumably dustless chalk—
on her desk, trees
cooked, matted, squeezed, dried, lined, and inked to bear
the twiggy thoughts of children

Mr. E.A. Poe is very definitely a
Romantic man its not everyday that
a crow comes a rapping and a tapping
at your window.

> *To me Thorow needs his head checked!*
> *Why would you want to give up headsets*
> *and phones just to think?*

This play was all talk!

　　: she stands
　　　　an apostrophe surrounded by all that is missing
　　　　a contractual question to be signed again on the respectable line

And her life was without name or clarity. And darkness was across her face.
Then the P.A. system spoke, wanting her presence in The Principal's Office
immediately. And the title of her day began. And the language dividing the light
from the dark will become her voice:

Waiting for Me

in his peppy green office, Mr.
Bright sits, surrounded by himself in pictures of prominent handshakes. Mr.
Bright never minds waiting, believing, as he does, in smiles, mission statements, measurable objectives, and shared expectations. He greets me—his voice
like a red and gold marching band playing out my name between the goal posts
of the home field. Mrs. Friche, he explains, will be arriving presently with
Jennifer, something about a research paper.

I am not surprised.

"Suck dick," Jennifer had said yesterday to my back after receiving her
grade on "Sex Change Operations," a three-page term paper hanging together
like a homeless person among twenty-some darkly photocopied pictures. After
class, she pleaded for a C . . . the paper wasn't her fault—a motel maid had
thrown away her notecards at the cheerleading competitions—her mother would
take away her car . . .

Wiping a tiny tear from her cheek, Jennifer enters
Followed by her mother
—a large endangered woman in a leopard vest.
Mr. Bright thanks us all for coming.
Jennifer asks him for a tissue.
"Effort," contends Mrs. Friche, "should not be failed.
Every night for a week," she declaims,
"This child worked at my dining room table.
Can you honestly say that's worth nothing?"
I discuss the lack of organization, transition, and support.
"But that's just one opinion," sniffles Jennifer, "lots of people liked it."
"The psychology teacher gave it an *A*," snaps Mrs. Friche,
"And the people at my office said it was excellent."
Mr. Bright, an ex-math teacher, smiles.
"Yes," he says, "grading themes can be subjective, but . . . "
Jennifer revives, cheeks pink as her Esprit sweats
The room becomes smaller, greener
Like the delivery room where failure was born
A great black fur mother eats reason
Into a footnote of hunger—all lost
in the exhaust of a red Miata . . .

I return to my room, compelled to the edge—
a line I am always outside

to the left and

One step beyond the school's right to them
They light each other up
Hair-hanging easy dudes
Thin in faded concert shirts
   Sin after Sin
      KINGDOM COME   Reign in Blood
Say *Aah* and **Ram It Down**
     Books dropped at the
curb in onomatopoetic   **Fuckit**
Backs to their alley, a 7-Eleven graveyard
Of Big Gulps, Twinkie and frozen burrito wrappers
Shoulders curving like dark question marks
Into their tight
Buttoned-up
501 balls.

     on this line, darkness is mine
     order conceived not in heat
     but in predictability—
     on this line, anger is mine

                           to the right and

Across campus, youthful bodies
Circle, turn
     bodies
   drawn to each other
In the sometimes silent,
     sometimes breathy
Mathematics of heat

   Hey, you sexy boy
—read the note I found in the lost book—
I love all those little things you have
for me to play with. See you later!!
   Love,
   Kara

  I remain dark,
  walking my line
      lips   and thighs

  and skirts curving out of impious slang
  into my slender, eternally uncertain
  aspiration . . .

    penises like divining rods
    searching out wells of wet stars

  the more paunchy whims
  diverted to oozie pleasure pastries
  faces breaking into unkempt need

                    —real and
                    imagined ORGASM

                    everywhere
                                        EXPLODING

                    I step into this ripe soup—
                    my line before me as I go

                        MACHINE WASH COLD WATER
                         TUMBLE DRY LOW HEAT
                           COOL IRON ONLY

                                    * * *

Suddenly passion and death are the tardy bell
And I am pledging allegiance to the Republic of Laughter
Located in the layer of Now
Where all the flowers have been cut
And arranged in chapters
Where children laugh and sing
As if scissors had never been invented
Where dreams are maps pulled down the walls
Like window blinds, and we fight the Red Coats for Liberty
Or death and nearly freeze but win on Christmas Eve
When the enemy lets down its guard
"May I go wash my hands," Lynette asks,
"I just killed a moth."
I write a pass

          the bell and

The Mona de Milo

A tall handsome boy hands me his transfer slip.
"So you like the 'Mona Lisa'?" he says,
Surveying the prints above my desk.
"Why, yes," I reply, impressed by his interest.
"I think it sucks," he says.
"On what do you base your criticism," I ask.
"I saw it," he says, "and it's little."
"True," I agree, "but didn't you get
A provocative sense of the unconscious of Woman?
Perhaps even of archetypal wisdom?"
"Of course," he says without batting an eye, "but
Something worth that much ought to be bigger . . . "

     Once I asked why so much money kept going
     Into the Cathedral of St. John the Divine
     Why it didn't go into playgrounds and schools
     For the kids throwing stones at our tour bus
     "Who do you think you are?" Dad fired back,
     "Jesus Christ? I don't see you
     Sending your allowance to the Puerto Ricans."
     I left
     But met a pervert in the bus station
     And went home . . .

 "Then there's the Venus de Milo," he says,
"She doesn't even have any arms. What good is it?"
Time schedules itself into my day
Stamping its thin precise hand on my plans . . .
"Henry was still there," I tell the class,
"A rose light filled that August evening
As The Pond rippled toward me out of its secret source
Into this tiny Bufferin bottle . . . "
"Dang, man," he says, kicked back in his chair,
"You talk about him as if he's God."
Their laughter strips me from my eyes.
My answers remain questions.
Errors are expectations not entirely expected.
The calendar will soon say May but I may never.
Last year Hemingway won out over Fitzgerald

Because the sentences are shorter.
"Fly Fuck the Whorld," says this year's
Official Theme Paper Plane
As I leave another stone
At the door of each of their instant minds . . .

And a bell like the sound of one hand clapping

I keep Manuelita after class
Her father says the family must go back to Mexico
She wants to finish high school in America
Just one more year
She wants to be something
Violet sweater creeping up her tummy roll
She doesn't know what
"Please help," she had written at the end
Of her composition on "Self-Reliance,"
"My sister's boyfriend is cheating on her.
If I tell, I will hurt her
And also break the trust he has in me."
Manuelita is wrapped deeply in her loyalties
Hot and soft inside as a peasant grandmother
Her lips are fat
Her friends are thin and go with boys
On Saturday nights she braids dark wet strands
From their temples over their heads
Then pulls the braids so they dry wide and loose
This braiding is her pride.
One night her sister talked her into sneaking out
The boys were Mexican
Although the words were said in English
For this was an American thing to do
They went for a ride
That was all
Her sister came back later and didn't get caught
But she got her father's belt across her thighs
"The truth is always best," I say.
She looks up from the close world of her text
Fingernails like chewed moons
Tongue tripping over the language of freedom
A frightened piñata filled with honor
Everyone taking a poke.

The nets of morning begin to fray
Into the threads of evening
Still, I catch myself believing
The rope across the Valley of Thunder loves my feet
Suddenly the fractured air comes together
And my feet awaken on an invisible wire
Connected to a tardy bell

38

How All Occasions Do Inform

and to begin with the gift of a poem is to offer a bowl whose meaning depends on whatever is not:

The Aging Slam Dancer
for Joan Eve Trimble

Wearing white socks on their cocks
The band came, she explains,
To relieve the tensions of winter.
"People used to have ideas," she says.
Her dance is a slow anger
Slamming counterclockwise
In the circular pit
Hunger is desire
Money is now
Sex is a pistol
Here in this ghost map city
Her city set on a hill
Where thieves break in
Girls like thin, narrow doors
Closing themselves
Into guys big as doorways
Wearing chains
Ask, says the god of mammon
And you will find enemies to love
Seek, and your cloak will be taken
Knock, and the wind will rebuke you
"You can't win anymore," she says,
"Not even in the subcultures."
Eat, take
This is my mind broken for you
Drink, take
This is my soul
Running headlong
Purple lips and eggwhite vegematic hair
Over the cliff into the violent sea
The muses don't care
Swine turn away from pearls
God is a genuine black leather question
Answered only in pragmatic vinyl

Moths go mad in the flashing light
Her blood rusts.

Joan Cutuly

- > +   initially

:
A few aren't sure
Most, though, think he's vastly overrated
He talked too much, took too long
Made a mess of life
Lots of people have just as many troubles
You have to fight your way to the top
A real hero would find a way
          Let me know, I tell them,
What you think in thirty years—
Not, of course, close to getting myself off the hook
These thirty-three seniors about to graduate want action
Answers or blood
No, answers *and* blood
Aristotle won't do—no pity here
No recognition of potential greatness
Dying served him right
          In fact, they were all losers
The teens are breathing fast
"Excited about learning"
          "Involved"
     Ganging up on me, nailing
   me to all that's holy in my hands
Making gluck, gluck sounds
          Ophelia drowns
Ahhhhhhgk—Polonius
          dead again not even for
A ducat, Claudius playing with everyone, fucking Gertrude
Though only in their minds (this is the honors class)
Laertes freaking
          And poor Rozencrantz and Guildenstern . . .
Only Horatio had it all under control
Never got involved, now there's a hero!
I bring up the poisonous effects of evil

Dean, The Dean I call him, wants to know
What's the difference between a tragic hero and a fool?
"Poetry?" I ask
          provocative as a bare bodkin
being
     and not being
                    The bell rings
"When's the test?" they want to know.
"The readiness is all," I reply.
"Seriously," they persist.
"Day after tomorrow," I say, concrete as Fortinbras
Ordering the sweet prince brought to the stage,
Also likely, had he been put on, to have proved most royal.
The distinguished scholars depart like flighty angels.
I rest in my moment of silence, breathing the dust
Of their squared-off catharsis,
Sensing another ghostly message . . .
A man in black approaches   hovers   touches my head
Alas, he says, poor Yorick . . .

> *and she returns with the gift of a poem*
> *bringing me the sun on a wheel of spokes*
> *converging in emptiness:*

> ### Battered Teacher Syndrome
> *for Joan Cutuly*
>
>   Behold God's law
> upon his creation, for bitter
> glass blows into gentle eyes.
>
> Once desert valley now deserted
> for a vengeance bed to lie in,
> sleep my sacred Shoshone—your
> land is gone.
> White light sky—cloudless—only
> hazy heat and implosive sorrow.
> We leave a desert that has melted
> into glass.
>
> Alas is right, strange INRI: Burn
> on your glass cross you wretched
> rash intruding fools—
> We run to cold soft
> Sand, up the mountains and into
> the clouds, arms outstretched,
> naked

Flocks of Eagle Angels All, we
see darkness in a man who
dies in love.

            Joan Eve Trimble

        another bell

Field Trip to the Ocean

"So," he asks, "how was your little conference with my mother
    last night?"
"Fine," I say,
"We agreed passing or failing is up to you."
He shows me a poem for another class.
"A satire of violence," I observe.
"Very good," he says. "The others will fall for it.
I'll probably be tested."
"You may," I suggest, "forget how to be honest."
"That's a very good point," he says,
"I'll think about that."
I want to bash in his face.

Once I asked of his future plans.
"Power," he said without hesitation,
"I want power."
"Interesting," I replied
"But what will you do with this power?
What form will it take?"
An invisible veil fell from his face
He looked freckled and ten
"Nobody ever asked me that," he said.
"Oh, m'gosh," he said last week
When I collected the *Gatsby* texts,
"I'll bring it tomorrow," he promised,
"I'm writing myself a note."
I want to smash in his teeth
I'll lose if I ask again
I'll lose if I don't
Either way, I walk right into those eyes
Gray as the ocean
Tides and undertow
Just waiting for me to lie down in the sun
I move him to the back by the door
Citing his chronic tardies
"I understand," he says

Fingering his Yin-Yang medallion
Of jet and pearl

He is a dark mother
Between me and his small cornered self

                              The Players
                    tardy again
Talking basketball with the principal
A month ago they were part of the crowd
He shooed through the hall
Last night they took Zone
Yesterday the cheerleaders baked them basketball cookies
Today signs in the quad shout

TAKE STATE   **TAKE STATE**

              Imagine The Rule Book
              Without any letters
              White
              Perfectly right
              Mother of God . . .

        Think of The Rules
        Without any book
        Black
        Vitreous floaters
        Chips off the old mark of Cain . . .

The dean keeps patting them on the back
The counselors are talking scholarships
"Warning" I write on their eligibility cards again
They're barely pulling D's, down from A's and B's
"No sweat . . . "
"Fine by me . . . "
They smile, riding the crest . . .

        A pass, please, to the coach for pain medication,
        Last year's Achilles tendon injury.
        "Worth the risk?" I ask.
        "At least," the reply, "if it snaps again
        I'll know I went out fighting."

              Imagine the score
              Without any board
              Numbers released
              Into fireflies

        Now think of the board
        Without any score

The absence of light?
Or ? a star fallen inward . . .

+ < -
head shaved to a shadow

Except for the black clump
Like a lost sheep falling over his eyes
Rusty insulates himself in an Army surplus jacket
As if public education were a personal assault on him
Only when he is sure no one cares, does he look out
From the other side of eyes
That have seen his mother drink
And slur her life
With a man, snow in his veins
And hers
She's named their new twins Felicity and Chance
Rusty's father is dead
Shot point-blank
By Rusty's mother
Rusty covered his deaf sister's eyes
And closed his own
Not enough hands for his ears
Now he wears the sound in his face
Silence surrendering knowledge
To a point beyond itself . . .

White moons flower from my hands.
These moons are the voices of children
Distracted from the fall of Icarus
By a picture of the poet's face—
"He's all crumpled," says one.
"Toss him out," says another.
They want cosmetic gardens with no toads,
Criticizing this poet's hair, that poet's nose.
Only an occasional death strikes their fancy—
A head in the oven,
The taste and smell of madness.
Their metaphors are weapons of literalism
Against all systems feeding them a refried darkness.
In despair, I throw off my hands
Giving them back their voices—

"I see black roses everywhere," writes Gema,
"And everything is dark.
Everyone is dead for me.
I do not care about anything."
Then she goes back to sleep.
"The brain," writes Julio, "is mainly made of water,
And it starts to imagine how water can kill,
How water picks up an object just by looking at it."
Then he goes back to his con game.
"Sometimes," writes Nichole, "I cry the tears of warriors
Now trapped in Christian Dior tweeds
But most often I cry for Mother Africa,
For she must stand alone.
As her uncomforted tears become my own,
My body is racked in sobs.
But my tears are as unfallen raindrops."
Then she goes back to that place I am unable to reach.
"I wonder," writes Huy Dam,
"If the moon is cold like me
Because it did not know
Our small boat needed darkness
The day I ran away from my country.
But we made it past the sea's boundaries
With hunger and great thirst for two weeks.
Maybe the moon shows our way,
Maybe the moon is my mother
Giving me her gold ring
The last thing I see of my country."
Then he goes back to his math.
Bumming paper and pencil
14-carat rings on every finger
Antonio writes, "My Hero—
He drive a cold ass motorcycle
That tear up any desert
Like the damn man
This boy can drive like he the car itself."
Then he goes back to examining the gold
On his fingers black as the fabric of night

Their darkness is the light
I must eat with no hands

and the bell, a knot without rope

unraveled in a note
dangled like a noose

MS. CUTULY,

    Thankx for the little chat before class, you're the only person in the world that I know that I could have one of those conversations with so Thank you and I'm truly sorry for unconsciously trying to manipulate you.
                        Your friend,
                        Jeremy

    the late bell—a chalky shell
bared iridescent in death

Roads Not Taken

: assigned yesterday
due at the end of the period today :

      The incident that I experienced was losing a homeboy (friend) Esteban Aragonez in a neighborhood fight.
      He was stabbed in the back and head and after that they ran over him. I really don't know how many times he was stabbed, but I think it was seven. I think that he might be set free, because there is not enough evidence. To me, there was enough evidence but probably the police didn't do a good job about it.
      I saw one time on television the governor or someone from his staff saying, "Use a gun; go to jail." It should also be, "Kill a person; go to jail."
      Some people might read this letter in their newspaper, and won't care, but what if it was your friend or what if someone from your family got killed, and the killer would go free—how would you feel?
      I know this is a free country, but when someone kills someone else, this isn't a free country.
      So to all in this city: We have shed enough tears, so please let us unite and form a strong proud family, like we should be. This will be my road now taken, in planning to become a parole officer.

                          Jorge G.

                          Kristina
                          Period 4
      On Christmas Eve, my sister and I took a three foot tree to my mother's hospital room along with a stocking of stuff that I had done for her, somewhat of a tradition since my dad's death. I am not sure if she really noticed the tree was there. But the thing I will probably always remember is when I was opening the presents in the stocking for her, I opened the cheap one dollar sink strainer for her, and I said something like, "Look, we've wanted one of those things for years. Now the forks and stuff won't fall down the drain." My mom's eyes lit up and she got this huge smile on her face and said, "Oh, yah," the first thing she had said to me in about a week, and pretty much the last thing she ever said

to me. It's funny how a simple thing like that can make such a lasting impression on me, but I will never forget it.

On Christmas, we got there in the afternoon, Donna opened her presents for her, but nothing excited her like the strainer had done.

Then it was the night of December 29. Donna and I walked into the room to find my mom staring into nowhere and breathing real hard with her mouth hanging open. We were not getting much response from her at all. Every time I would go there, I would say, "Going water skiing today?" and she would either smile or give some kind of facial expression, but not this time. She was so boney and she looked dead. She did try to tell us something that night, but she could not talk anymore. When Donna had left the room, I stood next to the bed, and my mom reached out her hand. I held it for a long time, but did not know what to say. After being there a few hours, the nurse said there was not any reason to stay because my mom could die any minute, in a few days or even a week. We said our good-byes, and were walking out the door when my mom started trying to say something again. I went back in there, gave her a big hug, and said, "Don't worry, we will be back tomorrow to see you," and then walked out. She died the next morning at 7:30.

I feel like I have matured a lot in the past month, not feeling sixteen anymore, but more like thirty. I have found that if I either sleep or just try not to think about it, I am not depressed. But at the moment, I don't have time to be depressed. There is a whole apartment to go through and divide among the family. I get most of everything, since I will need it all in a year or two, so I have to be the one to go through all the closets and drawers. It is not easy. And with semester exams coming up, I have all the stress that keeps building. Plus I have to learn to drive in the next couple of weeks or I do not go to school. My mom's car is now mine, I just need to learn how to drive it.

When I consider everything I have inherited, the money being saved that will end up being a few thousand when I get my own place, and the fact that I will have to learn to rely on myself, I realize this will really help me in the future. They say you can always find something good in everything, but I still miss my parents.

Oscar M.
Pd. 4

My Choice
My choice in life took place before I came here. The choice was whether I stayed in my country Nicaragua, or come to the United

States because my life was in danger. My life was in danger because the government wanted me to join the Army whether I like it or not. If I wouldn't have join the Army the government was going to send me to the mountains where I would probably have starved to death. My choice that I made changed my life in the way that I'm getting an education and have a chance to become what I want to in Life. I wonder about the choice I didn't make because I think that my chances of being alive would have been 30 percent out of 100 percent. I feel that the choice I made was the right choice because I would have probably been killed by now. This is how I feel about the choice I made as well as the poem by Mr. Frost.

Walden

On this particular day, the gray skies released a concealed sorrow of rain from their deed of mystery and cleansed the earth. The weather etched in my mind a picture of a beautiful girl in white kneeling over a chord of torment. She wept her soft sadness but held back her heavy tears. Above, the powdery clouds surrounded and isolated me from the rest of the world. As I stepped outside, I was welcomed by a romantic caress of cold air. As I walked across the icy, wet cement I spread my arms as to embrace the chilly atmosphere; it made me feel renewed. I deeply inhaled the clean, virgin air. A strong feeling of purity overcame me. Not just purity of the body, but of the mind as well. I felt very innocent and very righteous. I looked out at the dark world I live in. How correct Thoreau was when he said life was simple.

Late at night on nights I cannot sleep, I often find myself thinking of what events have happened on the soil directly beneath my home. If I stood on the land my house was built on back in the Dark Ages and continued to through the course of time, what would I see? I believe that as man evolves and society becomes more complex, we slowly stray from life's simplicity. In the Dark Ages, man worried daily about staying alive and finding food to eat. Today we worry daily about what to wear to school and where to go for lunch. We are evolving into a dry, parched future because life's rich value is slowly wilting. Life is too synthetic and is losing it's flavor. Not very much in our lives is natural anymore. We must look upon ourselves and become simple again. Life's necessities will exist as long as we do. We only have to open our eyes and see them.

by Steve Kiraly

Chang Lee
period: 4

The Chinese School
Before I was in school in china. And my father is a teacher there. All the school were stop teach. All the teacher were stop teach. student were stop study. We just went to school play around. have fun. Most student always fighting. Broke the window desk and the chairs. As matter of the fact. The goverment were so bad. The goverment let the people do anything they want. So people got to much trible. such as they fight each another. refused to the teacher, some of fight with the teacher. make a fun and scorn. Because. they just came to school work learn and not pay for the school too. They all very upset with the teach and hate the goverment. too many people left the country.

% = *

back from 7-Eleven
car parked—
InvisaBeam set:

The brothers come on time
Which is half an hour late
Bust a move, the hotty's fine
Hey, homeboy, do you have a Live System

*"Please step back
you are too close to the car . . . "*

Yo bro
Are there any white boys here
Who think they're dope, chillin' stupid stuff
DJ Shit 'n' Scratch'll turn their tables sho nuff

*"Please step back
I am warning you . . . "*

Wipe the white foam, pass the sweet leaf
Bury that face slapped fresh with Eternity
Deep in those Poison tits
    Go for it   Push

*"In five seconds
the alarm is going off . . . "*

The music is a heart
Like the bottom of a whiskey bottle
The music is a straitjacket
Hysteria minding its own business

UHH! UHH! UHH! UHH!

You got to get a education
To help support our nation
Give 'em what they want
To get what you want

> *"Please step back*
> *you are too close to the car . . . "*

Put your name in the corner
And fill in the blanks
Would you rather be a forest ranger
Mechanic, or a florist

> *"Please step back*
> *I am warning you . . . "*

High hair
Absorbing the shape of the high rollin' medium
Beeper, Beemer, silk shirts
1001 British Knights

> *"In five seconds*
> *the alarm is going off . . . "*

The music is red
Blood on cement
The music is blue
A soul fallen from the region of flight

UHH! UHH! UHH! UHH!

> Tradition is a business
> The business of control
> A system all connected
> You get out of life what you put in it
> In   Out . . . Down   Up
> The syntax of colors
> The grammar of Fuck

If the straitjacket fits
wear it

===

Christy Keller
Pd.4

Choices

People make up their minds before their choices are given. I was waiting in the doctor's office for the outcome of my test. The day was windy and very cold. Just the type of day to find out if you are pregnant or not. The doctor called me into his office. He said your test is positive. The first thing I thought was, what am I going to do.

After I came home, I got to thinking that there are three choices to choose from. First of all I could get an abortion, or I could give the baby up for adoption, or I could keep the baby. Immediately after realizing these choices, I knew which one I would choose.

If I choose to have an abortion my worries would be over. No one would even know I was pregnant. I could go on with my life. But an abortion sounds so horrible. It's killing a human life before it has a chance to live. Is a fetus alive? Is my life more important? Can I live with myself if I do this? These are all questions I asked myself. Then I thought, I've made one mistake. Should I, or could I, make another.

I could carry this baby for nine months, go through the delivery pain and then after all that never get to see the baby. When a child is put up for adoption, the child is taken from its natural mother as soon as it is born. You never even get to hold your baby. Could I go on with my life not knowing where my baby is and if it was all right?

If I keep the baby I would have to give up my free nonchalant way of life. I would have a new responsibility. I would have to worry about a babysitter every day while I'm in school or work. I wouldn't have to worry about whether my baby is being treated right by its new family. I would get to teach and raise my baby the way I want it to grow up. I would become a mature, reliable mother.

My heart told me, as soon as I realized my choices, which I would choose. So therefore the choice was easy. Only the acceptance of the choice was hard. Whichever choice I chose my life would change. Everyone has choices to choose from every day. Their choices may not make as big a difference as mine in their life, but their hearts always tell them which to choose.

Mary
pd.4

The Lesson

It started out in curiosity of romance. It ended up I was going to have a baby. I was neither prepared or ready. And my boyfriend, the father, was scared. It would ruin our lives, he said.

I told nobody.

I just thought. Day and night. Arguments of everyone has a choice to Baby Killer. It was then I came to see how life is not that simple. Choices are not clear or easy to know what is wanted or right. Also, abortion is not cold blooded murder.

Maybe I just say this to forgive myself—the sound of a life, my baby, being suctioned from me. Somehow I know I did the right thing for my future is yet beyond me. And it must be paid for with a person that would have loved me. But I could not trust the child of my responsibility to the world of chance.

However, in bed at night asleep a wall of my life is missing.

This is the hardest lesson of my life. You are put in this world to survive. And you become your survival.

"44 words of Advice"
by Al - Alex - Alejandro
Aragonez

Pressure

The burden of physical and mental distress smashing upon one's momentum to reach the top, all the sturdy weight of social and economic imposition seeking constraint of circumstance. In all seriousness, the stress or urgency of matters demanding attention can become a big pressure.

Yin and Yang
Could this be Mobius?

The car is too far!
The cat is too fat!

$. \{ \} = [\;] .$

Johnnie
period 4
Well, you know my big decision, which was probably my mistake in telling you. This I realized last Thursday when I said, "Hey you're wearing purple." Then you thought you needed to tell me you're not gay—so I wouldn't get hurt. Thanks, but I'm cooler than that. Now I feel like a real idiot with you probably thinking I'm after you. Don't worry. You're safe.

If you don't want to write the college reference for me now, I'll understand.

My Birthday
by Rebecca C.

I got to choose everything for my sixteenth birthday. Decorations of pink streamers and balloons with everything to match. And my relatives came from all over. Then my friends came later to surprise me. Everyone brought presents! My boyfriend gave me a gold chain with a little heart containing diamonds. At night my father gave me a letter saying how he was proud of me. It was in a beautiful and lovely wood jewelry box he made with his own hands. It will always be the best day of my life.

(Actually, he is my stepfather and we always didn't get along. My biological father left when I was born.)

no paper from Robert McBride
        pale, pimply
        hair scrawled over his upper lip
        nothing to write
        no roads taken
        or not taken
        his eyes never laugh

with a pencil borrowed from me
quick jottings from LaMar
        (barbecued chicken wings under his chair)
        I either want to be a Pimp,
        or a nice teacher like you.

and the bell, abstraction of butterfly and mind
chart of the uncharted way

Lake of the Lonely

Lunch:

The children with gold veins
Drive in their nice cars to The Picnic of Fatness
Succulent breasts, rumps, shoulders, thighs
Turn on spits
Red juice crackling the flames of glee
Leaping about the open pit
The children wash down salads of money
With sweet wine from the lists of their longing
"Eat shit," they shout at the sun
Burning like the blood of their ill-conceived
And unborn,
The children of Everything Possible
Drinking dry the Lake of the Lonely
As with little shovels of red, yellow, giddy
Green chatter, they dig up splatches
Of the ticking time   pack
   pack
Packing it into
Friendly little castles
  of forgiveness

  She lingers after class, organizing her books
  I'm hungry, have a headache
  But Ewok is dead
  I want quiet, need to sit
  But her mother is also dead
  Lung cancer, four years ago, never smoked
  Her father smokes three to five packs a day
  Ewok was mean at first
  No wonder
  Dragged in by Animal Control
  Bounced around all day in a truck
  Slammed in a cage
  She never knew her real father
  Her real mother left when she was four

The owner let him run loose
He bit an unsupervised child
So soft and tan
He would always run in cute little circles
But stuck to her ankles when other attendants came close
She is seeing Leon again
He gives her presents and puts her down
Her father is seventy-two, doesn't want her driving
Or working
She hates him for smoking
Is on probation for slugging a friend who lied
Wants to be a vet or animal rights activist
Hates herself for seeing Leon
The counselor is helping her apply for financial aid
Will I help her write a letter to the editor
 I'm hungry, have a headache
Need to sit
But Ewok is dead
Quarantined six months while a judge decided
Then yesterday his cage was empty
She ran to the freezer
Let it be empty, dear God, she prayed
No Ewok
She ran to the Euthing Room
No Ewok under the covers   turned
There was Ewok in the tub
She had wanted to take him home
The judges don't even know the dogs
The shelter is bound by the law
The owner never came
I walk with her toward sewing class
I'm going to change things, she says
Her father quit getting the paper
Will I help watch for her letter

Back in my room, I open my lunch
Just sit.
Ewok is dead.

0 > +

: He comes early from lunch with a progress report to be filled out for his parole officer—new student last week, just released on inhouse arrest. "Some black dude," he says, "called me a Spic. I beat the crap out of him."

Why . . . ?

a
metallic
blue
O
against
his
twelve and a half
year
old
forehead
he
heard
a
click
closed
his eyes

nothing

opened
his eyes
the guy
smiled

before that
he only punked guys for milk and pencils

Parents . . . ?
They came to America for a better life
Peruvian and Sicilian
A legal secretary and a banker
They met in Peru
Had no sex before marriage
Never, he says, knew anything
He learned from Abuelito, the old one
In a wheelchair, six teardrops tattooed on his face
A guy stuck him in the back with a twelve-inch ice pick
The room was dark like an ancient story
The Latin Kings were dying out
So they got a whole bunch of women pregnant
But all the girls weren't pure 18th Street
And the gang name changed to Little Locos

The good-looking ones—like me, he says,
Are always the meanest

Kindness . . . ?
Forget it.
In junior high he was shy but fell in love with Ginetta
They lost their virginity to each other
Then he started doing it with lots of other girls
One day he heard Rex got devirginized by Ginetta
I wanted, he says, to stick her head in a swimming pool
I poured Coke all over her
It felt good
At home I remorsed for five minutes
Then laughed
It was just Pay Back

Other girls . . . ?
A girl always says, "I will turn you out."
So then I just have to show her what's up
I take her into the bed
And work on her for around three hours
Then I stand up and look down
And she understands
She is my girl
I love her
We make love
She cooks for me
I buy her things

If you have a daughter . . . ?
If I have a daughter
I will worry every guy is the one taking my little girl
That they're in some room doing the wild thing
I'll put surveillance around her twenty-four hours a day
But always knowing there'll be some sly guy like me.
So I think now if I run into a jealous father
Will he give me a break
Snap my neck in three
Or maybe blow me away

Guns . . . ?
Hey, it's a business

I still got connections with a legal arms dealer
Had a great buy before I went up
A small terrain tank
Quite reasonable
A couple rich guys bought it for fun
You know, knock down a few walls and some trees . . .
Now as far as efficiency and expense go
The semi-automatic AK47 is your best bet
The Russian type
I could pick you up one tonight
For around seven hundred
And I'd throw in a scope and three clips
Plus a 45 semi-automatic . . .
Me—I like a 57 Magnum with a long nose barrel
Packed with 375 Magnum 44 grain hollow points . . .
I make my own
You put the shell on a little round stool
And weigh the powder in a little grain scoop
Then just pull down the lever of the bullet maker
To seal it all up—
He demonstrates the motions
With hands that are sensual, graceful, and precise—
Go a few grains over, he adds, and you'll pop the barrel
Or it won't even clear the chamber
And blow up in your face

WHY . . . ?
Well, a person makes you mad
So you let him have it
You wipe the blood off your knuckles
And you're laughing
It attracts a person when they know the excitement
Of running some guy up and having the cops chase you
Or a guy comes up to you, and you have
The one thing he needs
"Hey, man, come on, man," he begs.
 "Shut up," you say, "or I'll bust a cap in your ass."
The main thing though—you gotta stay clean
An established guy who starts on the stuff
Will turn into a scummy bag of bones
And a young, fresh mind is right there

Ready to move in with a posse that'll cut you up
And leave you all over the city
You can't be thinking of anything
      not food
      not sex
      not fun

It's kill or be killed
I'm still always looking around
Will somebody from my past come up after English or Math
And give me a pencil in the back
I've done a lot of shitty stuff

      But . . .
      but
      nobody's going to kill me
      no animal is going to eat me
      it would be ungraceful
         unmale

                                            the bell

The Lesson of the Pomegranate

They stare at me from narrow rows
Speak in thin steel letters
Dress darkly
And joke about driving by my funeral.
My job is to unite their fingers of flashing knives
Into a circle of brightness.
I have been educated to speak in mirrors designed to deflect
Their horrible light into an Illumination of Faith.
For months I have seen only myself down the long fluorescent
Corridor of one stillborn dream after the other.
But somehow today I see
The eyes of The Narrow Ones are themselves mirrors
Designed against the sun of all myths . . .

Suddenly a small red voice speaks
As from the edge of all sleep:
"There is a kind of mathematics to the human heart—
A transcendental ratio of myth to passion
A mystical rhythm of blood and air."

I look deep into the eyes of The Narrow Ones
Take from my lunch a pomegranate.
"I offer you this fruit," I say timidly,
"So cool and sweet, and red as the heart
Believing in sun as the mind of earth and rain."
I slice the pomegranate slowly with a small silver knife
As in a ritual of serving,
Sensing behind the mirror eyes
That small excited laughter of new leaves.
Many express the desire to partake of . . .

A Βελλ

transcending the imperishable
syllable of Brahman

It is my mirror polishing period, but I sketch instead
A figure roughly the size and shape of a human fist
Four darkened chambers made red
By the ardor of their own pulsing
Tones shaded into the sweet seeds of trust.
I take it immediately to The Person in Charge.
He leans toward me
With the ponderous ardor of an old elm.
"There is," I explain, "a mathematics to the human heart."
As I describe the vision of the red voice
His walls of Leadership Certificates begin to shimmer.
The sun in my mind rises to high noon.
"I love it," The Person says.
"We've got to make this a priority."
He sends me across the hall to

The Next Highest Person in Charge
Who listens with the classical reflection
Of an Ionian column.
"There is a mathematics to the human heart," I tell her.
She slides a calculator from her top desk drawer.
"No," I say, "I'm speaking metaphorically."
She replaces the calculator
And scans the index of her Poetry Handbook.
"Try negative capability," I suggest.
She tells me about a paper she did on
Keats   a nightingale
Suddenly enters the conversation   invisible   no,
Trapped in its invisibility   Time slows into
A drowsy distancing detaching me from myself . . .
"I like your idea," she says abruptly
And with the speed and efficiency of a teletype
Sends me down the hall to

The Human Heart Commission.
The Human Heart Chair listens, feet propped on his desk
A sign tacked on the wall that says
            Thank You For Holding Your Breath
                        While I Smoke

He takes a long drag
And flicks his ashes into a Pepsi can.
I show him the vision of the red voice.
"A flow chart," he says, "very impressive.
We'll send it to Graphics,
Have it copied for district-wide dissemination,
Mounted into an overhead for The Board, then . . . "
"Wait!" I say. "This is not what I meant. It's mystical and
Sweet, the intimacy of personal transformation . . . "
I despise myself for babbling.
How could what was so clear sound like a theory
Conceived by chimps?
"Of course," he agrees, touching my hand,
"And with you heading up The Pomegranate Project . . . "
"Please," I beg, "this is not what I meant . . . "
He pushes a button on his telephone.
The Person in Charge rushes in to congratulate me.
Contempt forges my frustration into a thin steel anger
But The Next Highest Person is tying a red helium balloon
To my wrist. It says CHAMP in big black letters.
"No," I insist.
"Well, at least think it over," says The Person.
"The team needs you," says The Next Highest Person.
The Chair files my drawing in a folder marked HOLD
And lights up

        back in my room, balloon loosed and fast to the ceiling,
    I pray into fingers of flashing knives

      and the final bell—
    precision colliding with momentum
  as the moon drags the oceans across the night
slowing the earth to a measurable objective

The Test

The ReACT Practice Test

This is a *ReACT* practice test. It contains
questions from a *ReACT* test recently
administered and is provided
to help you prepare for your *ReACT* test. You will need
good self-esteem, one mechanical pencil, and two Snickers bars.
Good luck.

STOP!

Do not go on until you are told to do so.

Go on.

The English Test

DIRECTIONS: In the Postmodern Impressionistic drive toward Excellence and
    Jump-*!-
        starting
           the Economy >>>
    Take the Pepsi Challenge
        By choosing the alternative you consider to be the BEST
    Then circle the letter of your answer.

                Stop when you come to the word **STOP!**.
Do <u>NOT</u> *Go on* until you are told to do so.

STOP!

Go on.

1. Which BEST describes Arthur Dimmesdale's girlfriend?
    a. kinesthetic learner
    b. ho
    c. Aqua Net Chic
    d. social fuck
    e. overachiever

2. In the opening scene of *Oedipus in the Hood,* to whom does the Oracle at South Central L.A. attribute the cause of urban blight?
    a. Jimmy Cap
    b. Mack Attack
    c. Sensimilla
    d. Home G Skillet
    e. U-Mutha Fucka

3. How does Oedipus greet Old Blind Homey?
    a. What up G?
    b. Yo.

c. Yo bro.

d. Hows it hangin dude?

e. I'ma gank me a ride an bail to the crib.

STOP!

Go on.

4. Name the HOTTEST item on the charts today.
   a. Rap
   b. Hip Hop
   c. Death Metal
   d. The Hanford Rad
   e. Public Enemy

5. Which would you be LEAST likely to find in the graduating class of your school?
   a. metal head
   b. base head
   c. dick head
   d. department head
   e. head games

6. Select a synonym for pig.
   a. posse
   b. player
   c. roller
   d. head banger
   e. Big Daddy Hot Pump

STOP!

Facts about the iris
Do not make the iris open.
              James Galvin

It means sort of if your kept in the dark you don't know what is truly happining around you. You should open your eyes to the truth.

The unknown truth about the eye is you don't make your eye open it opens by itself the unique way it opens make it different from anything else. Because you don't know its opening.

Facts about life will not be important to you until you realize what is go on in the world around you. Open your eye to realty.

Information doesn't make you understand. Information isn't knowlidge.

Go on.

7. Among the new words and phrases found in the O.E.D. are yuppification, clone, break dancing, nuclear winter, blow (as in leaving), basket case, brain dead, badmouth, acid freak, right-to-die, drunk tank, foxy, AIDS-related, passive smoking, cheapo, ghetto blaster, desktop publishing, bottom line, Eurobond, crack, buyout, drag queen, palimony, and the pits.

    Which teacher training workshop would be MOST likely to address these additions?
    a. Strategic Reading for the Middle School
    b. Integration of Entrepreneur Skills with the Curriculum
    c. How to Read Body Language
    d. Grief Education K–6
    e. WordPerfect

8. Which would offer the BEST practical hands-on experience to a low-efficiency learner?
    a. Hard drive
    b. First down drive

    c. Drive-in
    d. Drive by
    e. Driver's ed

9. The MOST appropriate administrative response to the rising tide of illiteracy in American schools would be to
    a. bust a move.
    b. bust a nut.
    c. take a step to the left.
    d. offer the Five Finger Discount Incentive Program (FF-DIP).
    e. obfuscate.

10. The method employed MOST often by state legislatures in funding public education would be
    a. statistical malapropisms.
    b. impervious correlation of entropic memo strategies.
    c. kinetic vacuums.
    d. artificial insemination.
    e. cruise control.

11. In The New World Order, time is
    a. money.
    b. of the essence.
    c. imaginary.
    d. an aphrodisiac jacket.
    e. the stream to go a-fishing in.

12. Select the sentence which is correctly punctuated.
    a. "Helen," asked Troy "what do you think of the Model United Nations?"
    b. "Helen," asked Troy, "what do you think of the Model United Nations"?
    c. "Helen, asked Troy, what do you think of the Model United Nations?"
    d. "Helen," asked Troy, "what do you think of the Model United Nations?"
    e. None of the above.

STOP!

IMAGIST POEMS ESSAY, HOW THEY REMIND ME OF

How lonely I felt, don't know what reason. Confusing, missing my family for years and years. Tree grow up and it looks differ. I wish that my family will stay the same, so I will be able to recognize them. Now I don't know where I am miles and miles on the earth felling alone, seeing different faces and don't know who they are. So hopeless I don't know what it is, that destroyed hope, Here come my positive mind telling that I should creat something good—to study harder, your friend offering you, take all the good to complete your need.

I remember one night I had a dream, my mom was in my dream, but I didn't see her face, "Imagist—" like canary's bird just begin to have a nice family, all the suddenly the wind just blow them all to the air, some blown so for away, some sticked on the mother's wings. Some drop on the ground so hard and they died.

The last thing that I remember about my mom face was with full of tears looking straight in my eyes . . .

Go on.

with rainbows I cover the name
of Claudia Quintanilla
she saw her best friend Freddie
hacked up and strewn with his family about their house
still she is going back to Salvador to be with her mother
and now her friend Chan Soeurn alone again
at five taken by the Khmer Rouge from her family
and put into a work camp
escaping she wandered the blood and bones of strangers
crossing, after two years, the Thai border into freedom . . .

now there is no war here where I am
only me trying to cover up
names on abandoned notebooks
for those who cannot afford their own—
teacher of American, that terrified language
of star-spangled endeavor
the red, white, and blue wounds of the pure
dying for power
it's a strange dinner we eat here
a sumptuous light

that trumpets through us
oh say can you see
we eat and breathe it raw or ripe
over the brims of our appetites . . .
"Pizza," he writes, sitting in his blind spot,
"is a state of mind"
"Cut off the hands of the time-keeper," she cries,
a single white line casting a shadow upon herself.
windows look in at those looking out at them,
time is dying into place,
and I am dying with it

STOP!

The Reading Test

DIRECTIONS:
        Reality is opposed to the spirit.
      In the half language of freedom
    along the borders of burning names
  between the fields of bones
Read each of the following carefully, then select the BEST answer from the statements that follow.

As German prose styles tend toward sparseness these days
So patrons of tanning salons everywhere are bathing in ultraviolet—
      FRY NOW   PAY LATER
As Napoleon said, Each state has the politics of its geography
Scented or Unscented
Peanut or Plain
Low Fat   Fat Free
Classic or Lite
StayFree   Depend
Regular, Gel, and Tartar Control
Yes, the options can be overwhelming.
There are safe cars, luxury cars, performance cars,
Practical cars—but when sex moves from the private
To the open and a teenager becomes pregnant
That was then. This is now
     (plus shipping and handling)
So for skin that makes a clear first impression
Call this toll-free number
Ask about our Brief of the Month Club
Be all you can be—
One Giant Sip for Mankind . . .
The Heartbeat of America . . .
Job 1
#1
10 9 8 7 6 5 4 3 2 1 Lift OFF!

1. And now with all the pain relievers available today, what is the overwhelming choice of Americans for everyday pain?
   a. Mr. Goodwrench
   b. Working with icons in a DOS environment
   c. A gourmet dark chocolate cake air-expressed to any U.S. address in 48 hours or less
   d. *The Lost Writings of Jim Morrison*
   e. *The Lost Writings of Jim Morrison* (now in paperback)

2. Which of the following would make the best title of the passage?
   a. *The Return of the Anchovy*
   b. "Lighting Your Own Fire"
   c. *Lesbian Textuality behind the Marxist Cash Bar*
   d. "You Deserve a Break Today"
   e. "Strategies for Helping Students Apply Concepts/Skills to Real Life"

3. Identify the sociopolitical question addressed in the passage.
   a. When is a door not a door?
   b. Whose life closed twice before its close?
   c. How can we reconstruct Deconstruction?
   d. How would you like the police to investigate your miscarriage?
   e. How can you shave without the blade touching your face?

STOP!

Go on.

HOW THE BLUE PERIOD BEGAN
Toward the end of the meal, after drinking heavily
Casegamus places several envelopes on the table
(One to the Chief of Police)
Whips out his pistol, and yells at her
"This is for you . . . "
    (He shoots)
Then says, "This is for me . . . "
     (BAM)

He misses the easy woman
But not himself—   (10)
The last of his sketches dipped in boiling oil
Such began the blue cubed death of a century
A burial in two tiers:
Earthly weeping for the pale man with familiar black hair
Who ate freedom as if it cost nothing
Then rose from his winding sheets
Into an afternoon of red-stockinged women
Or black—
Music thrown on the ground of no flags
A transparent architecture freed   (20)
From the constraints of right angles
To unask that puff of cigar in the face
Is it more far-reaching
To live for art
Or to die for nothing?

4. Line 8 is an onomatopoetic representation of
    a. just doing it.
    b. a sound bite.
    c. the eternity of revolving interest payments.
    d. abstinence as the only form of Safe Sex.
    e. telling Japan your not illiterate.

5. Use of this onomatopoetic device only goes to show
    a. nothing outlasts The Energizer.
    b. enhanced fax conferencing will help you communicate more
        efficiently.
    c. prompt feedback motivates and enhances student performance.
    d. abstract elements stressed at the expense of the pictorial can be
        hazardous to your health.
    e. "If Raphael would return now with exactly the same canvases,
        nobody would buy a single one." (Picasso)

STOP!

Dear Ms. Cutuly

      Sorry it's been so long since we've talked, but the chemo is really getting to me. For the past two weeks, I've thrown-up two or three times per day, everyday. It really sucks! I got another blood transfusion on the ninth then antibiotics for a week, they load me up with blood one week then they kill it the next with a dose of chemo. I won't be able to go to school this semester either. I'm so bummed on that. As you can tell I'm not a great typist, yet, but I'm going to teach myself. My grammar and spelling are way off too because I haven't done too much writing lately. I hope you had a good New Year's Eve, I was sick so I stayed home and watched the Dick Clark New Years Special. He never gets old. I'm kind of giving up on *Zen and the Art of Motorcycle Maintainance.* It's moving really slow.

      I've been thinking about death a lot lately, not my death but death in general. IN a way I think death is overrated. I don't know if I can say that because I've never known anyone who's died. Maybe I should say my death would be overrated. It's just one of those things you take as it comes. I've been doing a lot of different thinking lately. It's hard to put in words, then I guess I'm not thinking clearly enough since I can't put it in words. A lot of times I wonder why young kids want to grow up so fast. I mean you ask them what grade they're in and they tell you they're two grades older. Why would they want to grow up so fast? They should enjoy their youth as much as possible. I guess they don't understand how different things become in just a few years. It's like the moment you're eighteen, people expect so much out of you, they don't understand that it really is harder growing up today than twenty years ago.

      I really miss talking to you, even though it was only a few short times. You are about the only person who understands the wacko way I think, I think.

      This new typewriter is really great, now I just wish I knew how to type. give me time and I'll be faster than the secretaries at Vegas. I guess I'm getting better because when I first got this I'd write a few sentences and be stoked with that, now I write full pages.

      This may sound kind of wack and I haven't told this to anyone, but I wasn't really surprised when I found out I was sick. Near the end of my senior year, I started wondering what I'm going to do with my life. I just knew school and that was it. I didn't know what to expect and for the first time in my life I was really scared. It seemed I always had a feeling I wasn't going to make it after school got out. Call it mysteries of the unknown or whatever but I wasn't at all surprised. Maybe that's why I'm being so mellow about being sick.

Well, the end of the page is coming too close so I guess I'd better say good-bye for now. I have to go to Vegas to take my final exam to get my diploma.

                                                    See you real soon,
                                                    Andrey

Go on.

Thus, seeking to serve the Wide Glories, I arrived at the Gate of the Patriarchs. The Gate opened. Scarlet and gold pom-poms filled the air. My name was spelled in glockenspiels—winning there was an ivory word, a word with teeth. The Principal Pal called me into his office, where he spoke in the high morality of keys, of libraries with no dust, and anger that is always grammatical. "Virtue is syntax; syntax, virtue," he said.

Then he unlocked a metal file case containing the picture of a flame-fierce dragon, scales like mighty shields. "Oh," he moaned, "the helplessness of us all against it, unable as we are to access the two-dimensional."

"Have you considered metaphor?" I asked, feeling it presumptuous, even trivial, to suggest illusion as the cause. But The Principal Pal had vanished, except for a smile which I followed to a large white room with one white desk. On it, my name had been engraved in gold. I looked out on a field of young dragon fighters throwing themselves through fiery hoops. On the side, their women fanned the flames, moving like tall grass in kind wind.

They were all so beautiful I wanted to save them, and gave my mind immediately to metaphors of valor. The walls of my room disappeared as I became all windows and sun.

Suddenly in the heart of that light, the dragon materialized. Fearlessly, though, I led, and the young men bravely followed me into the dragon's brain. The flame raged, but the young women of the windy grass sang us into luminous transcendence.

However, as I turned on my metaphor toward victory, I saw all char, shrivel, and disappear like photo albums and old news under a fallen star. The door to my room reappeared as iron. The room itself had shrunk to stone. Through a small high window, I saw bodies like burnt orange rinds.

I cried out in confusion, denying my guilt, begging forgiveness, reproaching the light. But the words clinked into tiny green shields about my feet, and a smile appeared before me as through the dim chill I heard, "Myth is syntax; syntax, myth."

6. This passage would most likely be found in a work entitled
   a. *Inductive Concept Formation.*
   b. *Developing an Administrative Vision That Is Clear, Succinct, and Attainable.*
   c. *Diagnosing the Needs of Your Students.*
   d. *Stress Management for the Classroom Teacher.*
   e. *The Evolution of the Weekend.*

7. The moral of the story is
   a. Be all you can be.
   b. Never mind.
   c. Burnout sucks.
   d. First Alert—Don't leave homeroom without it.
   e. The shadows on the cave wall might be your own.

STOP!

Go on.

Brandon
I could have killed you more than once—
Always talking out,
Wandering the room,
Tearing off my pencil eraser
To hold your earring that lost its back,
Then just as the class dipped into Walden Pond
Sporting your little key chain man
With penis that flipped up and down,
Pulling the knife behind my back.
I met your parents over that.
"Don't you want to be a good son?" the dean asked.
Your mother said despite braces and contacts
You never got over buck teeth and glasses.
Your father said he traveled so much.

I sympathized but wanted order.
You complied with the quiet of mountains
That take forever to die
And worked hard for a week.
I think of your fine movie star features
Plastered back and made up for the casket.
The day before you died, the class split for a debate:
"Do women mistake politeness for rights?"
"Brandon belongs with the girls," Roy said.
"Oh yuk!" squealed the girls.
"Jokes," they maintained. "Sorry," they said.
Usually you'd throw a book or sulk
But that day just stared, having begun, I think,
To empty your head of all assigned roles.
The next day the silence of the class so deep
No voice or hand could reach it—
Only one bewildered by the grief,
Our Vietnamese refugee
Recalling his neighbors murdered in the streets
By men he shot to save his father.
Within weeks he would be the butt of gibes
For having eaten dogs to stay alive.

Brandon, we are the questions
You answer
Buried with your Wildcat spirit button
Pinned over your breast.

STOP!

The Science Test

DIRECTIONS: Go For It.

1. Entropy is
   a. a venereal disease.
   b. Vanna White's hairdresser.
   c. the wine steward at Valhalla.
   d. mascot of the EPA.
   e. the tendency of the universe toward A Board Meeting.

2. To decrease entropy, you should
   a. flip it off.
   b. blow it off.
   c. get down.
   d. kick back.
   e. chill.

3. An eggbeater is an example of which type of machine?
   a. Free condom dispensers
   b. The wheels of government turning
   c. All the king's horses and all the king's men
   d. A chicken with its head cut off
   e. The one out of every three children trapped in the shell of sexual abuse

STOP!

Go on.

4. Without the Exclusion Principle, quarks would not form separate protons or neutrons. Neither would they join with electrons to form

atoms. In fact, all would collapse to form a kind of cosmic soup. We can therefore conclude:

a. James Joyce had a way with words.
b. "Real men don't eat quiche."
c. A dispute over whose turn it was to clean up the cat droppings ended in the fatal shooting.
d. Vocabulary lessons are more meaningful when you use a new word in a sentence with the student's name: "Sally, your little brother was recalcitrant when he refused to do the dishes."
e. Role-playing experience in conflict resolution will offer invaluable insights into emotional arousal management.

Go on.

5. One of these days you'll be able to play tennis without leaving your gameroom. You'll just put on a special computerized helmet and gloves which will create a three-dimensional computerized world around you. Computer experts call this type of artificial reality a virtual environment, *virtual* referring to what appears to be present but is not. Other virtual realities could give people such experiences as living as a molecule, a spotted owl, or their lovers.

What moral issue is addressed by this passage?

a. Taking a bite out of crime
b. Building "more stately mansions" for your soul
c. Obtaining your own Qwik and E-Z Ozone Patching Kit
d. Making educators more accountable
e. Finding Elvis

STOP!

To The Students Who Don't Want My Advice:

At last the charade is over—
They publicly state that they don't want my advice
I am free—free at last

Liberated by their not wanting
The lean strength of the world's literature
Wanting instead their cake of freedom
And eating it too
So now I am free—Whee! Free at last
To say let them eat cake
And grow fat
Being unable by mid-life to direct
Their own misdirection
Rolling out of control
Down the slippery slopes of life
And when the cake of their youth is gone
Let them eat anger, their own anger
As I have eaten mine
In this charade
Of being chipper and good-natured
In their narrow world of anger,
Resentment, and boredom—
Let them make their sad mid-life learning
Fun
While they long, as I do now, to go away
From the ill-conceived direction
Of believing in the sanctity of children
Longing, as I do now,
To lie down beside the mind of a cat
To go for a while
From being the eyes in a face of dust
Vanity assigned to exalt valleys
A wilderness searching for its voice,
To go away in no wind
Black as the bewitched Bibles of Salem
A weapon creating readiness
For the slink-run-faster-than-reflex
Kill
Walking at last with clean feet from my darkness
Into the place of no thumbs
The life created by Diana
To mock Apollo's lion
Night purring among vowels.

STOP!

6. Closed systems uniting increase entropy. And when two closed systems unite, entropy increases by more than two. So which of the following statements concerning random errors is INCORRECT?
   a. They are caused by faulty apparatus.
   b. They are caused by faulty apparatus.
   c. They are caused by faulty apparatus.
   d. They are caused by faulty apparatus.
   e. All of the above.

Firewatch

He thinks of me by flashlight
And writes to describe that day's mock assault
Up an unassailable hill. A 30 percent casualty rate
Is acceptable in his new world.
He also quotes me, though really Lao-tzu.
"To be frank," he continues, "when I was in your class,
I thought you were just a crazy lady babbling your gums off."
He sat right beside my desk.
His class was an unassailable hill.
Bored and sure, they took potshots at the world
And all its literature.
With their carefree 70 percent averages,
I was the 30 percent casualty rate.
Now he tells me about his confusion and certainty
Which he is learning there alone at midnight
Outside the barracks of Camp Pendleton are One.

Go on.

7. Consider the following:
   * Heat increases entropy.
   * Heat is expended to maintain order in a closed system.
   * Disorder increases because we remember time in the order disorder increases.
   * More heat is generated while trying to increase order.

So how can entropy be reversed?
a. Disband all committees.
b. Unplug all clocks.
c. Have your free lunch but don't eat it.
d. Have your free lunch and eat it too.
e. There's no such thing as a free lunch.

STOP!

Random guessing means you are unsure of the exact answer. Do not waste time on that kind of problem. Are there any questions?

Christa . . .

> *gone in that gigantic exclamation*
of vapors across the sky,
the lesson beyond breath we failed to expect—
> *death*
> *among the primal elements:*
air, water, fire, and human error . . .

I also dreamed of Space,
Washing my feet in the light of all daring,
Falling free through that grand silence
Into the word dust of Time.
But here I remain on my tiny mountain
Trying to get through the eyes of real needles,
A weightless groundling caught between the rows
Of Pop, Rock, Rap, and Hustle—
Children breaking before me
Like the edges of sharp stars.
My feet bleed over these glittering failures . . .
"Hitch your wagon to a star" was what I learned
Before stars got close enough to warn
We're only remnants of our elders.

STOP!

The Mathematics Test

DIRECTIONS: Now you are going to do some problems by yourself. Remember to read all the questions carefully.

1. In his May 1992 *New York Times* editorial, Richard C. Wade pointed out that of the 60,000 prisoners in New York state, 21,000 are illiterate. Within five years, 60% of the prisoners released will be returned to prison. In contrast, Japanese prisoners are not released until they are literate, and their recidivism rate is only 20%. Does crime pay?
   a. It costs $2,000 to teach an adult to read and write; $50,000 to jail one.
   b. The total number of five-card poker hands possible is 2,598,960.
   c. Allowing for different learning styles creates a win-win situation for everyone.
   d. In 1862, a forty-one-year-old rice hand with poor eyesight went for $675.
   e. Whether two events are simultaneous depends on where you are.

2. *NEA Today* quotes the Citizens for Tax Justice finding that the Rhode Island state tax for the poorest 20% is 50% higher than that of the top 1% of the wealthiest. What should Rhode Island do to avoid severe cutbacks in public education and social services?
   a. Get more poor people.
   b. Put the toothpaste back in the tube.
   c. Don't worry; be happy.
   d. Learn to read lips.
   e. Shop for the language best suited to their needs.

STOP!

> Educated guessing means guessing an answer when you are able to eliminate other choices as definitely wrong. Educated guessing may or may not help you. Your score will be based on the number of questions you get right, minus a fraction of the number you get wrong.

Go on.

3. The faster you go, the more time slows down. If you could reach the speed of light, time would stop altogether. However, when Joseph's meteoric career in the fast lane fell apart, he tried cocaine. Later, to escape the long arm of the law, he entered a 21-day rehab program. What percentage of the roast is fat?
   a. Call an NEA Ed Star Specialist for complete information.
   b. Barbie's real-life measurements would be 39-23-33.
   c. Consult "Creative Cooperative Learning Strategies for Interdisciplinary Hands-on Units in Homogeneously Grouped Middle Level Classrooms."
   d. Consult "Creative Cooperative Learning Strategies for Interdisciplinary Hands-on Units in Heterogeneously Grouped Middle Level Classrooms."
   e. Beef—real food for real people.

STOP!

The Return of Joan Eve Trimble

She has initialed her poem—J.E.T.—
And, flying low, cruises in from the past:
Last night she was at a red light
When an undercover cop pulled a gun
On two black guys who got out of their car
To yell at a drug addict for running them off the road.
(She knew he was a drug addict
Because "once you've been one you just know.")
The cop was driving a Trans Am.
The gun was not police issue.
Her poem, called "Dragons," is besieged
By the virility and hardness that come
From eating a heart a week.

Go on.

4. The world's rain forests are being destroyed at the rate of 50 football fields a minute. And now amid the cocaine epidemic, heroin is making a comeback, creating dual addiction and increasing the potential for spreading AIDS. Who ate the Cracklin' Oat Bran?
   a. Eddie Murphy
   b. Murphy Brown
   c. Chicken Little
   d. The Juiceman
   e. Saddam Hussein

STOP!

Go on.

5. Preliminary *Weekly Reader* studies show that 49% of sixth graders go home to "no one." And the United States ranks 21st worldwide in preventing infant mortality. What will it take to reduce the troubling realization that the new space station could require up to 3,700 hours of maintenance a year instead of the estimated 130 hours?
   a. Total Oatmeal
   b. Total Commitment
   c. Total Recall
   d. Fruit Loops
   e. Hey, how about a nice Hawaiian Punch?

STOP!

Go on.

6. Americans use 50 million tons of paper each year—about 580 pounds per person. The paper that four people use in a year weighs as much as a big car. All this paper comes from more than a billion trees. If all Sunday newspapers, including the comics, were recycled, we'd save some 500,000 trees every week. Can we say, then, that the B-2 bomber is more economical than paper airplanes?

   a. Yes
   b. No
   c. Each person has a language with him/herself at the center.
   d. The number of medals awarded for action in Grenada was 9,754.
   e. Time heals all wounds.

STOP!

Thoreau at the Kuwait Border

He wanted "to serve and see new stars."
Inside his latest letter, a picture:
Sand wider than the sky,
A train of distant camels silhouetted against the flare
Of a setting sun that had not yet begun my day,
The laughing boy so thin he wore layers of shirts
Now handsome, hard and tall in desert fatigues
M-16 and helmet in hand
Gas mask strapped to his side.
He remembers "The Walden Project,"
Each student assigned to live for a weekend
With only the essentials.
"As you can see," he writes, "all here is the beauty of simplicity
But the details and responsibility of my job
Are eating away my life." He is among those trained to care
For the victims of chemical attack.
He looks straight and dark into the camera
As one who knows the enemy better than the enemy knows
   himself.
Those eyes are also

Mine.
Instead of turning up the heat
I pull on another sweater
And pray they will never stop coming back
To pick up the wounded.

Go on.

7. Fashion designers have discovered a way to make all furs from
   sable-to-squirrel reversible. Interfacings, linings, and construction
   are eliminated to create coats of incredible lightness. However,
   when you look out your window, the distant mountain is both
   larger and smaller than the window. What percent of American
   teachers, if they had it to do again, would not go into teaching?
   a. Zero cannot exist because it cannot be given any point without a
      measuring device.
   b. An identity is an equation which is true for all values of the
      unknown.
   c. Since there was a mist, how do we know the gorillas were there?
   d. **STOP!**   *Go on.*
   e. 24

STOP!

Go on.

8. If, when all is said and done, there is, as some physicists assert, zero
   energy in the universe, how can we reverse entropy?
   a. Party
   b. Party Hardy
   c. Dial-a-Prayer
   d. Reverse the charges
   e. Don't call us; we'll call you.

STOP!

Dear Ms. Cutuly,

    Greetings and salutations! It's just your former student checking in. Is the school system still as fascinating as ever or has it gotten worse? How is your writing coming? Well, I hope.

    Life here at Occidental is hectic but rewarding. I have finally gotten myself involved in several activities, and it has made a world of difference in my enjoyment of school.

    Now to my real reason for writing. I have decided that I am going to be . . . a teacher! School has taught me a lot about myself and the world I live in, and I came to the decision that as a teacher I could not only do some good for others but be happy as well. I want to thank you for showing me in both word and deed what it means to be your own person. I always admired you for your "allegiance" to yourself, and it helped me to see that who I am and what I want is important and that I should never sacrifice either of those things to try and please others.

    I hope this card finds you healthy and happy. Thanks again for everything.

Sincerely yours,
Page Benway

P.S.—My challenge to myself this year is, in the words of Cyrano de Bergerac, "to make myself admirable in all things." What a challenge!

Go on.

Author

Joan Cutuly began her teaching career in 1965, and her experience ranges from third grade through college in a variety of public and private schools. Her poems have appeared in *Desert Wood: An Anthology of Nevada Poets*, as well as in periodicals such as *Interim, Hyperion, Pivot, Arts Alive, Bristlecone, California English, Oklahoma English Journal,* and *The Comstock Chronicle.* She also wrote and hosted *Rhyme and Reason*, a thirteen-week television series on poetry sponsored by Robert Morris College.